THE
NEED
TO BE
GREAT

A. T. Schwartz

From the author of:

> *A Handful of Light*
> *Hearts on Fire*
> *Be Happy and Succeed*
> *Be a King*

~~~~~~~~~~~~~~~~~~~

CONTENTS

INTRODUCTION

A book wins approval when it accurately mirrors reality. I have tried to describe with this book, two realities. One is our lives, as we know them. The other is an ideal life – a life that can be ours if we will only want it.

All the character sketches in this work are part fiction, part fact. Even so, they are real. They reflect these two realities. While there are no figures in this book that I can point to and say 'that's Uncle Harry, or that's little Debbie,' this is only because I have not searched far enough or deeply enough to find them.

Maybe though, you know these people. Maybe they are one of your friends. Maybe you have met them in stores or on the streets. Possibly even, you see them within yourself.

PART ONE

A Friend
for Life

CHAPTER I

You are not alone

Let me introduce myself. You know me somewhat, but not well. I would like to change that now. I want to show you who I am, and what I do. Once I do this, I hope you will look at me as a friend. Then – if you wish – we can do many great things together.

Who am I? What do I do? I live half within you, half beyond you. The part of me that is in you occupies what people call the unconscious. From here, I speak to you. I send you messages. These messages you think of as ideas, impulses. I make suggestions to you. You choose to follow or ignore them. I advise you. You decide whether you like my advice or not.

In addition, I exist beyond you, in the world around you. I am in the people you meet. I am in the celebrities you hear about. I am in books you read and music you enjoy. I am in plant and animal life. From all around you, I send you messages. I show you different styles of living, different ways to conduct yourself. I bring you new things to look at, new things to admire – things you might even want for yourself.

An ideal

Everything you do, every word you speak, starts with a thought. This thought is a force. It has a power to make you act in a certain way. Even those thoughts that do not result in action, thoughts that just pass through your head, have an importance. They affect your personality in subtle but crucial ways.

What provokes such thoughts? There are a few such motivating forces. I am one of them.

Pictures

My job is to draw pictures in your mind. These pictures combine to form a portrait, a model of the person you want to be. You travel through life, and you collect such pictures. Step by step, you develop an image of an ideal person living in an ideal world. The values and goals of this image, of this model, are values and goals you need. They are the building blocks of your ideal. Introducing you to these values and goals is my job.

For instance as a young child, you see a firefighter. He sports shiny boots and yellow helmet. Expertly, he kills a roaring fire.

This sight inspires you. For days afterwards, you play 'firefighter'. You destroy great infernos. You boldly save lives. This game, this fantasy is my work. Here I introduce you to qualities such as Bravery, Skill, Public service, etc.

Then, as you mature, I shuffle these pictures. I show you heroes who are more complex, more rounded, more human. I mix for you the features of a number of people – the competence of one colleague, the friendliness of another, the stamina of a favored sportsman, the appeal of a special teacher, the wealth of a top broker, the glamour of a famous artist.

To this, I add historical and even fictional personalities. I spice your view with insights from the natural world. The strength of the lion stirs you. The grace of the deer intrigues you. The beauty of a flower, the calm of a forest, the power of a storm, all enchant you.

A friend you need

In this way, I do more than paint pretty pictures. Rather, I give you and every other person in the world, an example to follow. I give you a goal to strive for and a dream to dream. I urge you to achieve more, more than you presently achieve. I push you to be more, more than you now are. I motivate you to keep trying. I feed you with a reason to live.

"One minute, what's wrong with enjoying the moment, having fun? Is it a crime to eat and drink, to tell jokes, to sit around?"

Having fun is important. Still, reality tells us that fun is not always fun. Fun-seekers are often the saddest people you ever meet. The reason for this is that it is no fun if you are no one. And even when you already are a 'someone', fun will not always satisfy you. You must move forward. Stay the same, and you tire of yourself. Never grow, and you become sick of life. If you have no conquests to conquer, no mountains to climb, your parties will become stale, and even desperate.

I must make it clear though, that I am more than ambition, more than a set of goals. I exist independently of you. Also, I am powerful. I have many abilities. I have a warehouse of gifts to give you, favors to grant you. I hope you will see this. I also hope you will understand that I am your friend – the best friend you will ever have.

Gain-pain

Sometimes your friends hurt you. This is true of me too. For when you do not do all that you can, when you stop trying, stop striving, I haunt you, I taunt you. Sometimes, even when you work hard, I torment you. I plague you with thoughts of inadequacy and failure.

Not all your discomfort comes from me. But some of it certainly does. Still, while I hurt you, I do so for your gain, for your growth. For without advancement, without progress, life really is dismal, dingy and dull.

Milton Wine has a vision. He sees himself as being a new world leader. He sees himself bringing peace and riches, success and happiness, to all earth's peoples.

In his reflections, Milton gives out food and medicine to the poor. He imports and exports industry and expertise from country to country. He urges progress. He fights laziness. He trains different ethnic groups to seek friendship, love, unity. He upgrades the level of justice and equity. He orders polite, clean, calm living. He destroys war.

Milton sits in a beautiful office – President of the World. A thousand assistants surround him. This is his operation station. It floats like a spaceship. Within minutes, Milton visits any country he chooses. Once there, he speaks face to face with nations and their leaders. He instructs them. He inspires them. He builds them.

This is Milton's dream.

Milton does not speak to his family or friends about his dream. They would think him childlike, naive. They would laugh. But Milton does not discard his reflections either. He believes they have a power. He accepts that they are a part of his self, his destiny. He knows that they give his life direction.

Therefore, Milton holds onto his vision. He treasures it. From time to time, he takes it out and reexamines it. He adds new details and subtracts others. He adjusts and adapts it. He enjoys it. Someday, someday soon, he will realize this marvelous dream.

CHAPTER II

The game

Look how excited people become over games. This applies not only to games they play, but also when they simply watch. What makes games so exciting?

The answer is winning. Winning is the flavor, the fun of games. Winning is what makes games sparkle. The players try harder. The crowds shout louder. The competition becomes keener. Everyone is more alive.

Conversely, what makes life tedious? What makes study dull? What makes work boring? You must say the same answer as before – that there is no prize to win, no competition to beat, no goal to reach.

But, one minute, this is not true. People study and work for a reason. This reason is their goal. This is the dream they dream and hope to realize. They toil to win. Why then are they not excited?

You must say, that while they have targets, hopes, dreams, schemes, they are not actively aware of them. They do not focus on them. They do not see themselves as winners or losers. They sometimes even forget why they are working at all. As such, their labors become a hard, heavy burden.

Bring me in

This then, is where we can work together. Let me point you towards outstanding achievements. Let me parade before you exciting exploits. That is my part of our deal. Your part is to strive towards them. I will supply the idea. You hold onto it, remember it, focus on it. I will toss you the ball. You run with it.

See how every step of every day leads you towards your dream. This will make that step vital, important, exciting. This is true whether you are waiting for a bus, paying a bill or washing your feet. It is true whether you are selling goods to a customer, listening to complaints or romping about with a child. It is true whether you are toiling in the heat, suffering through a long meeting, or hitting your head against a wall. Any situation can be thrilling. Just give it meaning.

Let me make life more interesting for you. Let me boost you. Listen to me, and you will reach your dream in a faster, cleaner, easier way. Let me encourage you. Hold tight to me. We can fly.

At the top

Look at outstanding players play. Watch super sports people perform. You will notice that they focus totally on their game. They look only to their target. All their attention is to their goal, and they totally ignore the crowds. This is what makes them stars. This is how they excel.

Top players, whether they are in commerce, academics, music or sports, dedicate themselves. This dedication helps them shoulder many burdens. It turns a long, dull, distressing chore into an easy act. Their job does not bore them. They see how it brings them closer to victory – and they fulfill it with joy.

Let me, I beg you, enter your conscious thought. Know me. Learn me. Meditate on me. Let me change your life forever. I can alter your entire life in a delicious, energizing way. I can make it better than it ever was before.

Lara Gardner was quite indifferent about school. She held her own somewhere between halfway and the bottom of the class. Doing well in lessons, homework, tests, was just never important to her. Being at school at all was never important to her. One day a talk with Dad changed this.

"I'm sorry to tell you," said Dad, "that the day you finish school, I stop signing the checks. I cannot afford a higher education for you. So, you had best start thinking what type of job you want."

"Oh no," Lara thought, "I don't want to go to work at seventeen. I want college, and culture, and good times. I want new horizons – horizons beyond my family's dull, dreary lives. What will I do?"

So, Lara wrote to the schools for a scholarship.

"What I need," she told herself, "is not an ordinary grant. I want a super-grant. I want a grant that pays for food, lodging, clothes, books, and gives me pocket money!"

Lara threw herself at her studies. This was difficult, especially at first, but she focused on her goal. Whenever, she felt tired and discouraged, she trained her thoughts on that grant – the grant she knew would be hers.

Lara pitched into her classes. As she did so, she discovered within herself new talents and strengths. She could think. She could write. She could invent. Moreover, she began to enjoy school. As she dug beyond the shabby, ragged surface of her program, she found material that fascinated her, that absorbed her. She saw shining lights, a glittering genius. She learned to love her work.

Lara Hill won the grant of her choice.

CHAPTER III

All you want

Know though that setting goals is not easy. It is not as simple as you think it should be. Why? Because there is a gap, a rather large gap, between what you think you want, and what you really want.

Imagine that you need to get home. So, you board a train and travel three hours to the South. Then you discover that you should have traveled three hours to the North. You are now six hours away from your true destination. It comes out, that you would have twice as well off, had you done nothing at all.

Similarly, you may labor daily for what you assume will make you happy. Then you discover twenty or forty years too late, that it was not what you needed. It was not what you wanted. You did not work towards that which could really make you happy.

Careless

People are careless about setting goals. As such, they mostly get them wrong. "If only I was good-looking," they say. "If only I was rich," they sigh. "If only I was handsome, and rich, and a good joke-teller – then I would have it all."

"Of course," they add, "I also want to be good and decent. I want to be caring, and loving towards others." With all this, they remain wrong. They attach big importance to small items, and small importance to the big items. Worse still, they forget the big items completely. They are like the little boy who went shopping for his mother. The only thing he remembered to buy was the ice cream.

Give people every item on their wish list. Then visit them in six months' time. Question them carefully. You will see that they still lack more than half of all they want.

Hungry

What then do you want? What is it you really need? This is to realize your potential, your full potential. You do not want just one aspect of who you can be, one face of your personality. You want the full range of all that you really are.

To realize your potential, you have to find your true self. For if there is any part of you that you can enliven, that you can excite, and you do not do so, you remain troubled. If you have inner needs and you fail to feed them, you are hungry. Ignoring these needs only makes things worse. As long as you do not attend to them, you will remain hungry. You will remain frustrated, bitter, even angry.

Miserable hero

Larry Forman worked hard to become a champion. He devoted himself, he toiled – and he reached his every target. Now, at forty years old, his coaches tell him that his sports career is over.

"But I'm a young man," Larry protests.

"A young man, yes," they tell him, "a champion, no."

Where does Larry go from here?

"Well," he tells himself, "I saved my winnings wisely, and I am wealthy. I can enjoy my retirement in comfort. But retirement is not what I want. I am a doer, an achiever. I can't just sit back and sip beer. My older years are also a part of my life. What will I do with them?"

Larry worked for many years. He labored for a specific target. He excelled. He became the star he wanted to be. Still his efforts did not lead him to where he wants to be. Larry must look now for other goals, new goals. In a sense, he must start from scratch.

Go-getter

Jane Nash is a financial wizard. At work, she has the Midas touch. All she touches turns to gold.

"Your future is bright," they tell her, "and getting brighter all the time."

Still, Jane is not happy. Not even half as happy as she thinks she should be.

Sure, she has the material trappings of the young and rich. She has a fine husband, handsome children, lively friends. She lives in a fashionable house. She wears exquisite clothes, elegant jewelry. She drives a choice car. She socializes, plays sport, and is popular.

Why then is Jane not happy?

Jane has needs that are not being met. She is hungry for something. This hunger hurts. She has ignored this hunger for many years already, but this does not help her. It will not pass away. It will not disappear. It must be satisfied.

But, there is a solution – and I have it! I can help Larry and Jane and every other kid in town to live happy, harmonious, humming lives. Stay with me and I will tell all.

I must warn you, it will take a little explaining, a little study, to hear my message. Once you hear it though you will see that I am truly the best friend you ever had. In the meantime, and for me to succeed, you must take me seriously. My voice is soft and quiet. So, you must listen carefully.

CHAPTER IV

An enemy

I must tell you something else before we go on. This is that there is another force in this world with similar strengths to mine. But, unlike me, he is your worst enemy. He poses a danger to us all.

Of course, he loudly denies what I have just told you. He will tell you with all sincerity, that he has your best interests in mind. This too is one of his tricks. He is a liar and a cheat. He will gladly rob you of everything you own.

Still, handle him correctly, and he can be extremely useful.

Slave-master

Who is this underhanded character, this foxy foe? I call him SLAVE-MASTER. The reason for this is simple. When you stay on top of him, he is your slave, and he serves you. When however, he dictates his wishes to you, when he commands you, you become his slave. You serve him.

You need to control SLAVE-MASTER. If not, he will control you. Do not let this happen. For should he become your master, should he enslave you, he will degrade you, disgrace you, and ultimately destroy you.

Desire and lust

SLAVE-MASTER is a force that dwells inside you. He takes the form of desire and lust.

Like every animal, humans have a survival instinct. They search for food and shelter. They fight or flee from predators. They create homes for themselves and fill them with family and friends.

However, unlike every animal, food, leisure and other sensual acts do not satisfy their human desires. On the contrary, the more they fill them, the more they want. The more they indulge their physical, carnal hungers, the hungrier they become.

Animals living in the wilds, eat when they are hungry, and stop eating when they are full. With humans, this rule changes. With their superior intelligence, they search constantly to fill their cravings in new, delicious, luxuriant ways. Today, they may settle for a slice of bread, but tomorrow they want it with butter and syrup. Today, they may enjoy a hunk of meat, but tomorrow they want it with fried onions and mustard.

Then, even when they have butter and syrup on their sandwiches, and fried onions and mustard around their steaks, they are not happy. So, they continue to search for new, exotic pleasures.

This is not only true with food, but with every material and emotional need. If they have money in the bank, they want it doubled, and doubled again. If they have good houses, they want them to be larger, grander. If they have lovely wives and charming husbands, they want them to be more stunning and glamorous. If they have audiences of a hundred, a thousand, they want them to be ten thousand, a million.

The problem

"Well, what's so bad about this? Surely you also spoke loudly in praise of ambition and striving, just a short while ago?"

The problem is that the more people feed their desires and lusts, the smaller they become.

When people act with greed, with selfishness, when they grasp, snatch, squabble like beggar children, when they snarl, spit, shriek like alley cats, they degrade themselves. They act in small, stupid ways, and they become small and stupid. Their stature shrinks and shrivels, decays and dissolves. They lose their dignity and pride. They forfeit their glory.

Swim or sink

SLAVE-MASTER plays an important role in your life. If he were not to tell you that you were hungry, you would die of hunger. If eating food was like eating foam rubber, like swallowing beach sand, you would stop eating. You would lose strength. You would become weak and sickly and fade away.

SLAVE-MASTER however, gives you an appetite for food. He adds flavor and aroma to all you eat. He excites your taste buds and tugs at your salivary glands. Thanks to him, you eat.

But SLAVE-MASTER's ambition stretches beyond your survival. His fondest wish is to addict you to the joys of eating, to transform you into a compulsive eater, a glutton working his way through mountains of meat, wading through swamps of sauces and sweets. He wants you to think all day of food, to dream and meditate on it, to drool and slobber over it. He wants you to eat until you burst. He wants you to ruin your life in pursuit of this lowest animal urge.

Similarly, SLAVE-MASTER tries to rule you with all your physical and emotional needs.

A little wine is healthy and pleasurable, but he wants you to be a drunk.

Drugs have tremendous healing properties, but he persuades you to be a junkie.

Intimate relations play a vital role in your emotional life, but he urges you to become a pervert.

In every area of your life, SLAVE-MASTER seeks to spoil your life, to ruin you. You want to earn a living, to relax, to have fun. You want to gain acclaim, fame, to maintain your health and beauty. He looks to contaminate you, to corrupt you.

There are three modes of consuming, of taking from this world. The best of the three is when you take only what you need, the vital minimum. Second to this is when you permit yourself 'just a little more' – this is the area of allowable surplus. Third and worst, is when you indulge every lust and desire. Then you fall into a sewer of ugly, evil excess.

For your own health and well-being, you need to maintain restraint and control. SLAVE-MASTER however, prods you to greed and gluttony.

master of the master

Control SLAVE-MASTER, and he is a true, trusty servant. He helps you. He supports you. He promotes you. But, fall in love with his charm, his allure, and you become his slave. You lose your freedom. You surrender yourself to an animal. You commit suicide.

> Bill Carroll walked through his forest. He liked to stroll after his heavy lunch, and he liked his forest. He did not spend much time in his mountain resort, so when he could get away, he took advantage of the opportunity.
>
> Bill Carroll felt especially good that day. He had spent the morning thinking how he surpassed his millionaire father in so many ways. While he had not quite matched the old boy's fortune, he certainly topped him in his standard of living. An army of servants and services attended to Bill's every wish and desire ... and Bill certainly knew how to live richly, royally.
>
> Suddenly, he noticed a man, sitting quietly under a tree, gazing at the view. His clothes were strange, but his face was serene, dignified.
>
> "Who are you?" Bill demanded. Bill was normally polite, but this was his property. Surely, he could know who walked it.
>
> The man looked slowly at Bill. Then, looked off into the distance and answered, "I am your master's master."
>
> Bill was a strong man. Still, the man's words struck him forcefully. It took him a few moments to calm down.

"Are you trying to insult me?" asked Bill, narrowing his eyes. "What are you saying?"

"I am saying," said the man, "that you are a slave to your lowest urges, your animal desires. You yield to your every wish. You obey your every whim.

"I, on the other hand, control my desires. I am a master over my lusts, my passions. This makes me a master of your master."

CHAPTER V

Greatness

"Well, you've made a great deal out of what a good friend you are and how much you can help me. You have also told me about your competitor, SLAVE-MASTER. But you haven't told me who you are!"

Until now, I have been shy of attaching a name to myself. The reason is that I am afraid you might misread me. I especially do not want you to laugh at me. Still, I must expose myself, and I will do so. Only please, I beg you, take me seriously. This is bigger even than ten million words can describe.

My name is GREATNESS. My design, my function is to give you greatness – true greatness, real greatness. I feed you greatness; I clothe you with greatness; I satisfy your 'need to be great'.

Follow me, and you will grow. I will give you wealth and power wider than the oceans, heftier than mountains, richer than rubies, sweeter than fruit and honey. I will give you the nobility of kings and queens, an excellence that no one can touch, that no one can take away from you. I will give you greatness that is yours and only yours, the dearest possession you will ever have.

Be great, and you gain satisfaction. Be great, and you gain serenity. Be great, and you gain success. You taste a success beyond anything you have never known.

Towards greatness

To become great is different to buying a car or a coat or a candy. This is because when you buy a car, you have a car. You buy it once and it is yours. But greatness is limitless. There are ever-new levels to achieve. As such, it is the best target of all.

When you strive to reach a certain goal and then you reach it, your striving must stop. You cannot pursue what you already possess. This inability however, is a great loss, a tragedy. It robs you of your highest pleasure.

Imagine you have a tremendous thirst. You have spent many hours toiling under a sizzling sun. You have sweated hard. Now you are as dry as desert sand. Your body screams for water.

Just as you feel you might faint, you receive a glass of frosty water. Look how it glitters, like a diamond. See its clarity, like crystallized light. Feel its coolness, fresh as a summer breeze. Listen to its music, the icy cubes that tinkle against its sides. Then drink, and drink, and drink. Is this not an ultimate pleasure?

But a great disappointment awaits you. For once you quench your thirst, once you remove the ache, the pang, the scream, the water loses its heavenly flavor. The glinting, glimmering goblet you held, becomes a finger-stained piece of glass. The water in it, is now just water – plain, tasteless, everyday water. The pleasure has gone.

What you need is a constant craving – a thirst you can water without ever being filled, an enjoyment that goes on and on. Can such a thirst exist? Yes, it can exist. It does exist. It is your thirst for greatness.

This thirst, this need for greatness, is a gift. But you must cultivate it. I can introduce you to greatness, but you must make it your goal, your dream. You must focus on it, meditate on it, internalize it.

Take this gift. Hold it carefully, consciously, as you would hold a gold bar or a pouch of pearls. Follow the path to greatness. Seek greatness. Pursue greatness. Make greatness yours. Be a great person.

Saul Bick is a master carpenter. His every item of furniture is a work of art. Saul has been producing his pieces for many years, yet he continues to work with a passion. He seeks always to create more flawless, exquisite, ethereal products.

The experts acknowledge Saul to be a leader in his field. His pieces fetch princely prices. Yet, Saul has little interest in wealth or fame. His mind focuses on harmony. He wants to create furniture that mirrors the grandeur of the forests. He concentrates on producing works that have the delicacy, the intricacy of the great symphonies. He toils over them that they may reflect the strength and solidity of the mountains, the glory and majesty of the seas.

This does not mean that Saul is unhappy with the work he has already produced. He also enjoys the publicity and payment his labors earn him. Still, he longs to produce better pieces. This craving, this love, is a fire that pushes him ever further along a path of creativity and invention.

Saul Bick strives for greatness.

CHAPTER VI

Shifting horizons

The beauty of pursuing greatness is that the horizon forever changes.

> Stand at # 14 Northfield Avenue, and you can see all the way down to # 55. After that the road twists and is lost from sight. Stand at # 55 Northfield Avenue, and you can see all the way down to # 99. After that the road twists and is lost from sight. Stand at # 99, and you can see all the way down to # 147...

It is the same with greatness. When you are small, you have a certain vision of greatness. "This is great," you say. "Nothing else can match it."

If you make no move towards this greatness, this remains your viewpoint of greatness all your life. But when you move towards this greatness, when you make it yours, you find suddenly that your perception changes. You see something new. You see something different. You see something you never before imagined.

This is the spiraling world of greatness. As you reach one level, you see a new one, a new horizon. And as you reach for this new greatness, again you see a new greatness. Your horizons keep shifting.

Is this not discouraging? Not at all. For the pleasure comes from filling your thirst – not from killing it.

A new you

One of life's great pleasures comes from finding something new – a new gadget, a new necklace, a new hotel, a new friend. The greatest of all these pleasures however, is discovering a new you. You experience your greatest joy when you renew yourself.

You are your working ground. You are your life. You work on yourself, and you reach your highest creativity. You work on yourself, and you draw out hidden strengths. Even as you work for others, you may improve yourself. Even as you earn your wage, you make self-gains – you acquire new skills, new knowledge.

You explore, improvise, and your life changes. Your world grows more dynamic. It turns over. As you move towards new ground, towards expansion, you feed that deep hunger within you. You feed the hunger that stirs you, pushes you, agitates you, all the days of your life.

"I teach computers at the school," says Sue Chilton. "This is my official position. But I use my classroom for more than computer science.

"Nearly all my students have one hang-up or another, and since my classes are small, I make time to go through their problems with them.

"Normally, we pick a topic like 'freedom', or 'insults', or 'stuffy parents', and work it through. The findings of these discussions are amazing.

"As we probe the topic, as we exhaust it, new issues open up. Unusual tracks of thought appear, and we crash through jungles of worries. Then, just as it seems that we are ending our search, a whole fresh area opens up before us.

"The kids get very excited when this happens, and romp merrily through these new fields of thought. They gather armfuls of fresh, sweet suggestions...

"I have been holding these discussions for many years, but our work still moves me. The more I invest in these children, the richer our discoveries become. I even use the solutions we prepare in my own life...

"I get a special joy from watching these kids grow, seeing them turn from nasty, self-seeking brats into fine, sensitive people. I also get a special joy from seeing how I have grown, how I have changed from being nasty and self- seeking, into a person who feels and cares.

"Imagine how different my life would have been, had I learned this way in my teens."

CHAPTER VII

Setting goals

Greatness is about reaching goals. However, greatness is a general term. You need specific targets. What should these be?

To be great has more to do with who you are than what you do. Still, it is 'what you do' that ultimately decides 'who you are'. Therefore, to become great, you need to plan carefully what to do with your life. You have to make planning a priority.

In five, ten years

A powerful tool in planning your future is this: Imagine yourself in 5 or 10 years' time. This is not the pessimistic picture you see whenever you feel low. Rather, this is how you would like to see yourself in 5 or 10 years' time, how you would enjoy seeing yourself in 5 or 10 years' time.

Imagine this with all the details. See yourself at home. See yourself in the garden, in the house, at your desk, in your kitchen. See yourself at work. See the type of work you are doing. See the people you work with. See yourself at play. See yourself with family and friends. Create an full picture of the person you would like to be. Formulate it carefully.

Three lists

Write down the ingredients of this picture. Do not hold back. For instance if you see yourself as moneyed, and driving a luxury car, write them both down. Although 'moneyed' includes the ability to buy a car, you want a clear, life-like picture. You want to launch your imagination. This in turn, will launch you on a path of real change. So, list everything. This is your LIST A.

Now, calculate the type of person you need to be to satisfy your hopes. Look here not only at education, skills or credentials. Look more at the type of person you are. And in seeing your person, look more at your personality traits than your physical features. For greatness depends more on the type of person you are, than what you look like.

Pinpoint these qualities, and write them down. For instance, if you see yourself as a leader, write down the traits that you need to be a leader –

forceful, trustworthy, knowledgeable, etc. If you see yourself as a friend, mark down the qualities that friends have – loving, giving, supportive, fun.

Take every face you wish to wear – child, husband, wife, parent, teacher, tycoon, artist, author – and identify its features. Create accurate portrait of all the different people you want to be. Write down the qualities each one of these people has. This is your second list, LIST B.

Now, study LIST B, and from it work out what activities you should engage in, how should you spend your every day. What preparations should you make to build the person, to create the individual you wish to be. This is your third list, LIST C.

Think of the three lists as follows:

LIST A: Where am I heading – what do I want from life?

LIST B: Who am I – what sort of person do I need to be?

LIST C: What am I doing – how am I getting closer to my dream?

Len Chaplain has a terrific picture of himself in five years' time. He has a solid business – he and 10 assistants are producing the newest interior designs in the city. He has a pleasing, attractive wife and three cute children. He lives in superior suburbia, a wall-to-wall paradise of good taste and comfort. He has a group of good friends and they spend a few chummy hours together each week.

That is LIST A. Now for LIST B ...

As a good interior designer, Len needs to be a person who is sensitive to the moods and themes of the world around him. He understands human nature, and knows how to help others relax and feel happy. He works well with his workers and gives them orders that they can easily follow. He also leads by example, focusing on all that he does.

As a husband and father, Len needs to be caring. He gives time to his wife, listening and discussing her issues. He plays with his children, urging them to be the people they need to be. He enjoys his family, and celebrates their many achievements.

As a friend, ...

But one minute Len, before we get involved in lists B and C, we need to go back to LIST A, and make some changes.

To be great

Nowhere on Len's LIST A was there any mention of greatness.

This means that Len has devised a list that cannot lead to his happiness. He has a plan that cannot feed his potential, that cannot satisfy his hunger. Len has ignored this important truth of the human condition. He has disregarded a basic element he needs for life.

Len must rewrite his grand plan, and not forget that magical need, that source of all pleasure – his need to be great.

CHAPTER VIII

Different levels

"Okay, you tell me I need greatness. I need greatness to replace unhappiness with happiness, dissatisfaction with satisfaction. I need greatness to fulfill my potential. How am I supposed to be great?

"And, before you start ... Who says I'm not great already. My friends tell me what a great person I am. Doesn't this mean I have greatness?

"I also want to know, with all this talk about greatness, do you want me to change jobs, careers? Do I have to be the president of the U.S. or the president of the world to be great? Aren't you writing this book for everyone? We can't all be world leaders!"

What is a 'world leader'? If you define this as seeing your face on the first pages of the finest journals, then to be a world leader is definitely not for everyone. Also to be a world leader then means you are famous, but not necessarily that you are great.

However, you can understand the term 'world leader' differently. You can say it is someone who contributes something unique to the world. He improves the quality of life for others. He inspires them to live at higher, happier levels. In this way, he 'leads' the world towards a new goodness, a new excellence. He inspires and takes them to new success. This is certainly great.

Great already

Your first question, 'am I not great already', is also important. Moreover, the question becomes stronger when you point to the fine, noble acts you do each day. Since these acts have some effect, some influence on others, you are already a leader.

You and every other person on this earth, have greatness within you. Many of the acts you do each day are kind, humane, virtuous. They are grand, glorious, even amazing. Many of your moments shine like suns. Still, greatness is a goal to strive for constantly, every hour, every minute. You have to reach out for new acts of greatness, new words of greatness, new thoughts of greatness. You have to continually become a greater person.

The pursuit of GREATNESS is an ongoing task. There are millions of different levels. This however, is not your concern. You need to reach for the greatness that lies just beyond you, the greatness you just cannot reach.

Great acts

There are earth-shattering events that are great. There are small everyday acts that are great.

There are people who hold important jobs. They affect tens, thousands, and even millions of others. They certainly do great things. Their greatness though is not a true greatness. It is the greatness of their positions rather than the greatness of great people.

Then there are great individuals, people who act in fine, high-minded ways. Such people stand straight, tall, with dignity. They are calm, certain, without being cocksure. They are in control of their selves, of their lives, but not arrogant. They are alert, active, looking always to learn new ideas. They are stable, content with their world. They are happy. Others respect, admire and even love them. The greatness of such people comes from doing small everyday acts that are great.

Martha Sender is a woman of principles. One of her principles is she does not give gifts to beggars. She is happy to lend a cup of sugar to a neighbor. She will loan money to a friend, and even close an eye when the debt is 'forgotten'. But when it comes to beggars, her door is firmly closed. It offends her that such people should clutter the streets and annoy upright citizens. It annoys her that they do not look for jobs and live in an orderly way.

Last Tuesday, Martha walked her usual route home from the market. Her basket was a little heavier that day. She had decided to treat herself to some freshly baked tarts. These certainly would enhance the tea she planned to drink when she got home. Suddenly, she felt a tap on her elbow.

"Please Miss, I need some help, just a few coins..."

Martha turned with a stern expression, and saw a gaunt face. It was a face that looked hauntingly familiar.

"I know you from somewhere," Martha said. She fumbled in her purse for her glasses, but when she looked up the beggar had disappeared.

Martha returned home in a shaken state. The face she had seen was a face from her schooldays, the face of a best friend.

"Could she have fallen so low," Martha wondered, "what could have happened to her? I remember her as such a cheerful, happy spirit. What has happened? Where is she now?"

Martha rethought her principle about not giving to beggars. It took a shocking event to help her change her mind. Still, the decision not to judge others, to look at them with compassion and concern, was her decision. It was her act of greatness.

CHAPTER IX

Add to yourself

What constitutes greatness? What makes you great? If you spend two minutes blowing up a balloon, you are you plus a balloon. You have invested two minutes of your time, of your life, into a balloon. As such, it is a part of you. You are everything you were earlier, and you are also a balloon. You are larger. You are greater.

Similarly, when anyone or anything receives of your energy, of yourself, he or it becomes a part of you. Give of your time and strength to a certain cause, and you expand. You become a part of that cause. Give of your focus, your concentration, to someone else. To some extent, you become that someone else. The more you invest in others, the more they are you.

But...

The problem with balloons is that they burst. Does this mean the two minutes you invested just died?

No, not if your balloon spreads a little joy. A balloon that makes a child laugh, is a balloon that lives on. A balloon that brings a smile to a teary face, is a balloon that uplifts the world. A balloon that infuses new hope into a sad soul, is a balloon that is great. If you give your two minutes to such a balloon, you have made a great investment.

Give your time to blowing balloons, and part of you is balloons. Give your time to planting a garden, and part of you is a garden. Give your time to caring for a horse, and part of you is a horse. Give your time to encouraging people. Plant your beliefs in them. Comfort them. A part of you then, is in these people.

Give yourself to others, and their success becomes your success. Give yourself to others, and their growth is your growth, their gain is your gain. The more you invest in others, the greater you become.

Investments

Where should you invest your time, your thoughts, your money?

It depends what return you are looking for. Do you want to make money? So, invest your time, thoughts and money into money. This is the way to make money.

Do you want comfort and luxury? Invest your time, thoughts and money into searching for comfort and luxury. Then you will find comfort and luxury.

Do you want greatness? Give your time, thoughts and money into becoming a great person. Then you will have greatness.

> Mike Ross did not care too much for study. He was not looking for high-flying careers. So, when he finished school, he took the first job that attracted him. He became a bus-driver. The work was easy and pleasant. Mike enjoyed chatting with the passengers, and he felt he was helping others by getting them to work and school on time.
>
> But over time, Mike became increasingly unhappy. He felt a deep dislike with where his life was heading, or rather, where it was not heading. He took some comfort in his 'after work' beer and newspaper, but he knew that this was a refuge, an escape from his gloom.
>
> "What's wrong, Mike?" a friend asked him.
>
> "I don't know," answered Mike. "The job is good. The pay is good. My family is all well. My home is comfortable. There is more than enough going on in my life, more than enough to keep me busy..."

Mike has many fine qualities. One outstanding trait is that he is satisfied with his lot. He is not crying over the size of his house or the model of his car. He is not complaining about problems within his family. This we can admire.

Still, Mike needs something. That something is a mission, a goal he can strive for, a future that is bigger than his present. Mike needs a greatness he can grow into, a glory that is all his.

Mike has a strength he is not using, a vigor he could be exploiting. Maybe a weaker member of his family could benefit from a particular talent of his. Maybe a local school or club could gain from special skills and abilities that Mike has.

Think, Mike. Think. Look for a way to realize your greatness.

A grave affair

A yardstick for greatness is the tribute you will receive at your funeral. What will they say about you? More important yet, what will they not say about you?

This yardstick is a guide. It tells you the type of greatness you should work towards, the goals you should list in your plans for the future. You can extend this idea further by imagining a news article or even, a biography of your life. What would you like others to write about you? What are the highlights they should point to? Make these reports and descriptions your target.

No one at your grave will say what an elegant house you lived in, what handsome clothes you wore. They will not mention how comfortable your armchair was, or how much cheese and pasta you ate.

They will however, mention that you were a loving husband, wife, parent. They will say that you enriched the community, helped orphans and widows. They will comment on how you strove to clean the world of abuse, poverty, ignorance. They will cite how you toiled to increase human dignity, tolerance, peace.

If you blow up balloons for your own pleasure, they will not speak of this at your grave site. But if you blow up balloons to give happiness to others, they will engrave it on your tombstone.

Strive for greatness, and help them write that tribute now.

Part 1, in short...

(i) The visions of greatness you see in your mind, the dreams of glory you dream, are a force. They help you set goals. They help you keep growing.

(ii) Set goals for yourself. Focus on reaching them. This will make your life more meaningful and exciting.

(iii) You achieve little, and even move backwards, when you chase the wrong goals. Know clearly which goals will lead you to happiness and success.

(iv) Do not let SLAVE-MASTER, the force of lust and desire, rule you. You must feed your physical and emotional body, but this is not an end in itself. It is only a means to keep you healthy and fit.

(v) Your true need – once you have food on your table and a roof over your head – is the need to be great. Moreover, it is a goal you can strive for all your life. Therefore, make GREATNESS your goal.

(vi) When you move towards greatness, your view of greatness changes. It develops.   It   expands.   Thus,   it   is   a   goal   that forever challenges and energizes you.

Work on yourself, and reach your highest creativity. Draw out hidden strengths. Explore, improvise, and your life changes. Move to new grounds, and feed that deep hunger within you – your need for greatness.

(vii) How would you like to see yourself in 5 or 10 years' time? Make plans to reach this dream. To do this you must know (A) what you want from life, (B) what sort of person you need to be, and (C) how you need to spend your time. Make sure that being great is part of this picture.

(viii) Your great acts make you a leader. With them, you influence others to live at higher, happier levels. To maintain this leadership though you need to seek always for new ways to improve yourself. Do great acts; and what is more important, be a great person.

(ix) Give of yourself to others. Thus, you become a part of them. Give of yourself to others, and you become greater. You are more than you were before.

What would you like people to say about you at your funeral? What would you like them to write in your biographies? Make these qualities your life-goals. Strive for them.

PART TWO

You and your World

CHAPTER I

waiting

Tomorrow morning the sun will rise. The alarm clock will shrill its way into your night. Garments will be waiting for you to wear them. Toast and coffee will be there for you to eat. Transport will be on hand to carry you forward. Life lies before you. Do whatever you want. Go wherever you wish. Accomplish whatever you like. You make it happen.

You have a problem though. This is your desire to take life easy. Lie in bed an extra hour or two. Be lazy. Stop thinking. Stop trying.

This desire urges you to wait for things to happen. Wait for the telephone to ring and bring good luck into your life. Wait for your bosses to give you a raise, to promote you. Wait for your lottery ticket to shower you with the grand jackpot. Wait for others to pour love, laughter, fun, over you. Wait for success and achievement to enter your world.

Well, this desire is right. You must wait for things to happen. But first, you must do all you can do yourself. You must plow, plant, harvest, grind, sift, knead, bake. Then you can enjoy that sandwich. Then you can expect that stuffed turkey to fly into your mouth. Make every necessary effort, every intelligent attempt. Then wait. Wait with anticipation. Wait with courage. This is the path to GREATNESS.

From around you

What the world gives you, depends on how you look at the world. Focus on that which is beautiful, and you will aspire to beauty, you will aim for beauty. Look at that which sings and smiles, and you will sing and smile. Look at that which shines, and you will shine. Enjoy the glory of the world, and the world will trumpet your glory. Feel the power of the world, and become a part of this power.

But, look to that which is ugly, dirty, mean, miserable, and you bring out the dark side of your nature. You set the background for misery – the growth of your lowest urges. Look to that which is wretched, which is vile, and your gut releases within you black juices. It oozes secretions of self-pity, stinginess, spite. It spouts wellsprings of anger, revenge. It bubbles with depression, despair.

Gifts

Did you mold your heart? Did you assemble your mind, or one of your eyes? Did you knit together the nettings of nerves that run through your body? Do you know how to mix chemicals and produce a kernel of wheat, or a chicken? Can you fabricate wood, stone, iron ore?

Almost all you and everyone else in this world has, comes to you as a gift. Your share in your own wellbeing, is a grain of sand on the beach. Your contribution to all that makes life worth living, is a teardrop in an ocean.

Your organs, limbs, sight, hearing, speech, touch, smell, are gifts. Your ability to think, to progress, the parents, friends who raise you and care for you, are gifts. The folks, the places that surround you, embrace you, the objects you use and enjoy, the food you eat and leave over, the billion and one items that make up your life, are all gifts.

See these gifts. Be grateful for them. Then, show your gratitude by using them in the best possible way.

Rejoice

When you waken in the morning, see that you have your intellect, and rejoice. See how you can open your eyes, move your limbs, stand. Say now: This is a great world. The sun is shining. There is air to breathe. There is floor under my feet. Enjoy it.

Feel the greatness of the world, and step in time with the world. Synchronize yourself. The world gives pleasure to others, and so do you. The world inspires, challenges, asks people to do more, be more, and so do you. The world is a source of energy, movement, joy, and so are you.

You emulate the world's vigor and beauty, and others emulate your vigor and beauty. They see your enthusiasm, your energy, and they follow you. This is the path to GREATNESS.

"Look Mommy. Look how the leaf skips across the ground, how it whirls and hops and rolls away. I can also whirl like a leaf. I can roll. See me roll Mommy, away and away and away from you.

"Look how big the sky is, Mommy. Look how wide it stretches. I can also stretch. I spread my arms wide, as wide as the sky.

"Look at me jump, Mommy. I almost touched a cloud. Look again. Did you see how I almost touched the cloud? If I jump really hard I will touch it. Next time I will touch it.

"Look at me squirrel, Mommy. I can squirrel to the top of that tree. I am holding. I am climbing, fast, up, up, up the tree. Aren't I as fast as a squirrel, and bigger too?

"I like this park, Mommy. It's fun. Can we come here again?"

CHAPTER II

Get wise

There is wisdom in the world. Some of this you understand. Much of it is beyond your probe, your grasp: the movements of galaxies, the forces of the universe, the workings of organic material, the properties of inorganic material, the nature of life and death, of birth, of growth.

There are ideas you have learned and forgotten. There are ideas that you have never learned, but that others have researched and written about. Then there are ideas still waiting for someone to discover them. This knowledge challenges you. Come and learn me, it says.

When you understand your world, its workings, its secrets, you can do more. When you study the design of the world, the lay out of the human body, the human personality, you can be more.

Read the writings and reflections of great people. Think, meditate, contemplate, and enlarge yourself. Increase the power of your mind, and you move farther, faster.

Obtain new skills, and live more. Learn. Gain insight, understanding, knowledge. This is the way that leads you to GREATNESS.

Grow

When living organisms stop growing, they die. This is the nature of the world. Either move forward, or retire and die. This is true for you too.

As much as you accomplish, you dare not stop. As much as you acquire, you must have more. As much as you become, you must be more. For if you stop, you slide. You fall.

Can't I rest on my laurels? Yes, you can, but only for a short time.

Look at the peach. It starts out as a delicate blossom. Slowly its bud swells. Soon you can identify the birth of the fruit. It constantly gets bigger, rosier, lovelier. It becomes softer, and releases its delicious fragrance. It is a perfect peach.

Then it stops growing. And...? Well, unless someone eats it, it begins to shrivel. Bugs infest it. Its skin sags. Its body rots. And it dies in a heap of compost.

Only with growth, do you continue to be a vital, happy being. Only by striving, constantly, can you continue to live, and enjoy.

When Peach Stuart married his beautiful, talented Dianne, his happiness was complete. He loved her greatly. He was thrilled by her many charms. Peach however, was in for a shock. Dianne made his life miserable. She was forever bickering and quarreling with him. Then he hit on a wonderful idea.

"Dear Dianne, since you are my queen and so beautiful, I would like you to have the grandest house in the world. Phone estate agents, hire the best architects, the finest decorators, and create a gorgeous home."

Dianne was excited by the challenge. She threw herself into the project with all her talents and energies. Nine months later, she was ready to show the world the most heavenly house it had ever seen. All who saw Peach and Dianne's new home gasped at its magnificence, its majesty.

"We must have a marvelous housewarming party," declared Dianne. Peach nodded his approval.

Again, Dianne called on her energies and talents. This time, to prepare their party. And again, she succeeded with elegance and style.

At the party however, she noticed Peach looking quite glum. "What's wrong Peach," Dianne exclaimed in horror, "don't you like the party?

"Or maybe..." Dianne said clasping her hands at her new thought, "you don't like the house!"

"No," said Peach, "the house and party both dazzle me."

"So, why are you upset?" asked Dianne.

"It's like this," said Peach, "as long as you were busy designing and making first this house, then this party, you didn't quarrel with me, not even once. But now that your projects are over, I'm afraid that much heartache awaits me."

Create

Create, innovate, strive for greatness. Then happiness is yours. Do new things, or old things in new ways. Acquire new skills. Conquer new territories. Rearrange your house, your day, your world. Accept new challenges.

Do not just re-style your hair or move the living-room furniture around, although such activities may help to fire your enthusiasm. Rather, review your attitudes, reset your targets. Look at the world around you, and see how you can enhance it, beautify it. Innovate, create, and approach mundane chores with joy.

Keep inventing. Do not stop. For when you stop, when you rest on laurels, when you act king and queen, you will find much to dissatisfy you, to agitate and annoy you, to frustrate and infuriate you, and your life will be miserable.

Lan Pearl wrote beautiful music. His first album he composed in grim poverty. Frustrated by a tiresome daytime job, he devoted his nights to writing and singing his heartfelt songs. He poured all his tensions, his tears, his hopes, his yearnings, into his music.

When his first work was published, Lan achieved fame and glory. He also gained financial independence. He was not rich, but he could afford to leave his dull, painful job. "Now, you will hear magnificent music," Lan told the world.

His critics however, disagreed.

"His new works," they said, "are very clever. Still, they do not match the charm and depth of his first compositions. The emotion, the fire and desire, are missing."

The fame and glory that followed Lan's success, toppled him from his peak. Lan had made the mistake of resting on his laurels.

CHAPTER III

Applause

You live in this world. You interact with this world. You work and function according to the rules of this world. Your needs are fulfilled or denied to you by the world. This includes your need for greatness. It is the world that declares whether you are great or small.

Sometimes, people praise and applaud your great deeds. More often, they ignore them. Therefore, you cannot use their recognition and applause as a measure of your greatness. How then do you recognize it?

Your best measure is to look at the benefit the world gets from your activities. If you are enriching the lives of people around you, people near or far, this is great. If you are bringing meaning, direction, joy into their lives, this is great. If you are encouraging and supporting them, this is great.

Pioneer

You need also to examine the quality of your activities. How much heart do you give to what you do? Do your schemes fill your mind? Do your projects capture your imagination? Do they seize your attention, fluster your concentration? Does excitement race through your veins?

If the answer is yes, then this is great. When your labors occupy all your thoughts, this shows that you are doing pioneer work. You are forging new tools, devices that others will also use. When you exhaust yourself over your projects, you are discovering. You are exploring new territories. When you focus completely on your plans, when they fill your days and nights, then you are working in a great way.

Adoption

How do children belong to their parents? In a sense, they do not. One day, they pack their bags and leave. Still, in other ways, they certainly do belong to them. Parents feel a link, a bond, a love. They take pride in their children's exploits. They celebrate their children's successes. They cry out when they trip, when they fall. They fret over their education, their future. Why?

Part of this bond is biological. Children come from their parents' bodies. They are a part of them. This however, is not a full reason. We see how close adoptive parents may be to their children. On the other hand, we see real parents walk away from their children.

A better reason though, is that parents 'adopt' their children. They undertake to feed, clothe and care for them. They give hours and days to nurse them, to cradle them. They provide them their wants, their needs. It is these acts that make the children a part of their parents. Their investment of time, energy, effort, bonds parent to child in a strong, permanent way.

It is the same with other people. You can mother and father them like you care for your own children. You can undertake to feed, clothe and watch over them. You can give hours and days to provide them their needs. Your investment of time, energy, effort, bonds you to them like a parent to his child.

Make it yours

You live in this world. You interact with this world. You need to give to this world. As you give, you become greater.

This means that you must adopt some part of this world. Take some area, the houses on your street, or your town, or your country, and make it yours.

Look for ways to improve your world. Make it cleaner, neater. Make it more polite and friendly, more helpful and kind. Take responsibility. Work on it, and make it yours. The more you do, the more fulfilled you become.

David and Tracy Carr had just moved into town. With David off at work, Tracy felt overwhelmed, crushed. So much lay ahead of her. Her entire household was packed in boxes. Six tired, moody, nagging kids hung to her dress, and she had nothing to give them besides dry crackers. Where should she start? What should she do?

Then Tracy heard a knock. She peered through the spyglass to see sparkling eyes, a sweet smile and a huge chocolate cake.

"Oh dear, it must be someone lost – and of all people, look whom they choose to blunder into," Tracy thought to herself.

But there was no mistake. The cake, together with a welcome note and a helping hand, were for her. Tracy was the new girl on the block, and the block had just adopted her.

CHAPTER IV

Give and take

You live in two worlds. One is the world of giving. The other is the world of taking. They appear to be similar. But they are radically different. For one is a world of GREATNESS, the other is a world of smallness. When you give, you enter a world of giants. When you take, you enter a world of dwarfs.

> One minute, that's hardly fair. Surely we all have to take? Does that make us dwarfs?

All people take. As babies and children this must be. How could they survive if others did not give to them, did not support them? Even as adults, they take. Every transaction, every interaction, consists of give and take. All are takers and nothing can change this. True?

No, false. Children start out life as small people. They certainly need to take. Adults however, have the potential to be great. Thus, they have the potential to become pure givers.

The ice cream sellers

Every transaction, every interaction involves people giving and people taking. Still, those involved really have only one objective in mind. This is to either give or to take. We can illustrate this as follows:

> Gavin Palmer wants big money. He wants to be the first self-made millionaire on his block. He calculates that the business to make his millions, is in ice-cream parlors.
>
> Gavin finds a well located little store, where many people pass by. He sells at the lowest prices so that he can draw the largest crowds. He hopes also, that in this way he will smash his competition.
>
> Gavin plants a big smile on his face, and waits for the millions to roll in.

Although Gavin is handing out ice cream all day, he is really taking. Giving ice cream is just a means to make profits.

Barry Levell wants to help humanity. He wants the world to be a place of greater happiness, love, and respect. He feels that the way to enhance these values is to give out ice cream. He believes that if more people will eat ice cream they will be less irritable and more tolerant of their fellow human beings.

But Barry cannot stand on the street corner and give away ice cream. He needs freezers. He needs space. So, he finds a well-located little store where many people pass by. He also cannot afford to give away the ice cream. He must pay rent and other expenses. He must also feed his wife and kids. Therefore, he sells the ice cream at a profit. Still, he looks for the lowest price that will allow him to cover his costs.

Barry plants a big smile on his face, and waits for the people to roll in. He waits for them to take his wonderful cure, his marvelous formula against the ills of society.

Barry's main goal is to help his fellowman. He believes, rightly or wrongly, that the way to do this is with ice cream. Although Barry takes money for his ice cream, his essential interest is to help others. His goal, his thrust is to improve the world. Barry is a giver.

The doctors

Let us look at Gavin and Barry from a different angle.

Gavin Palmer wants big money. He wants to be the first self-made millionaire on his block. He calculates that the best profession to make his fortune is plastic surgery.

Of course, to make it in plastic surgery, he must have the highest skill and expertise. So, Gavin works extremely hard to pass all his courses with the highest marks. He makes a special effort to train with the greatest masters. He willingly does the most menial tasks just to be able to observe and learn from them. He volunteers for hospitalwork in the poorest districts. He knows that here he will build his skills. Here he will gain priceless experience in working on the trickiest and most lucrative cases.

"Later," he tells himself, "I will move to better-placed hospitals, and even private practice. Later I will make the fortune I want."

On the other hand…

Barry Levell wants a career where he can help others. He has read about the scarring of people through traffic accidents, war incidents. He has heard about the huge harm these scars inflict on the emotional health of their victims. He grieves for the plight of such people.

Barry senses that plastic surgery suits his natural abilities. It is a career that matches his intelligence and strength, and will challenge him.

Barry knows that to succeed in plastic surgery, he must have the highest skill and expertise. So, he works extremely hard to pass all his courses with the highest marks. He makes a special effort to train with the greatest masters. He willingly does the most menial tasks just to be able to observe and learn from them. He volunteers for hospital-work in the poorest districts. He knows that here he will build his skills. Here he will gain priceless experience in working on the trickiest and most sensitive cases.

"Later," he tells himself, "I will move to better-placed hospitals and even private practice...

One moment ... if Barry is such a giver, then why then is he looking to better hospitals?

"I know," says Barry, "that for my emotional health and well-being, I must maintain a certain standard of living – I must earn a decent wage. For this to be possible, I must work with well-to-do patients."

Still, Barry plans to give 10% of his working day to volunteer work. He is sympathetic to the plight of others, and he will look to exercise it wherever he can.

The seeming difference between Gavin and Barry is not large. They are both highly skilled doctors, doing the same work, under the same conditions, and earning the same wages.

Folks however, draw a line between them. Gavin they find, raises his chin at them. He has little time for the luckless. Those who know him better, see that under the veneer of courtesy, concern and charm, dwells a nasty man. Barry on the other hand, has a genuine affection for others, rich and poor. His courtesy, his concern and charm, is no veneer. He is plainly a good person.

Barry gives. Gavin takes. Barry is great. Gavin is small.

CHAPTER V

Host or guest

The next time you are at a party, ask yourself this: Who are enjoying themselves more, the hosts or the guests? Who are more active, more in tune, the hosts or the guests? Who are brighter, more spirited, more energetic, the hosts or the guests?

The answer (usually) is the hosts. Since they give more to the party, since they work harder for its success, they receive more than anyone else does.

A party

The world is a party, lavish, openhanded, free. But this truth has a condition. This is that you must first see it as being a party. You must convert life's toils and troubles into pleasures and more pleasures. You must make that which is difficult into part of the fun, part of the challenge, part of the amusement.

Play the game – do not stand to one side. Play the game and enjoy your life.

Roles

There are two roles at a party, host or guest. There are two roles in this world, host or guest. You and everyone else, must play one of them.

To be a host means that you worry that others have cake on their plate and a drink in their hand. To be a host means that you involve others in the conversation, in the party games, in the fun. To be a host means that you are giving.

To be a guest means that you worry only whether you have a cake on your plate and a drink in your hand. To be a guest means that you look that others should talk to you, award you prizes and smiles, feed you the fun. To be a guest means that you suffer through the party, and receive little pleasure or satisfaction.

To be a host means that it is your party. To be a guest means it is not your party.

Happy are you

An important part of being a host is to enjoy the fun and games. Although you must concern yourself with the needs of others, you do a better job if you too are lighthearted, bubbly, happy.

Also, when you are serious, sober, the guests take this as a sign that you are annoyed with them. If you show anger towards your waiters and cooks, they feel you are angry with them. This can dampen and spoil the entire affair.

Guest is host

Most of the time you start out as a guest. This does not mean that you cannot become a host. To be a host means to concern yourself with the well-being of the guests. Anyone can do this if he or she wishes. You need only to start looking to others and caring for them.

You are invited to a party? Bring some eats. Make a salad. Whip up a dessert. Buy a bottle of wine. Contribute, and become one of the hosts.

You are at a party, and it is dull? Sing a song – with the householder's permission, of course. Tell a story. Whether the story is absurd, romantic or sad does not matter. The main thing is that you are giving, you are contributing, you are being great.

You are at a party, and it is a mess? There are not enough people to serve the food? There is no one to clean up the spilled soup? Leave your seat, take a tray and serve. Leave your seat, find a mop and clean up. Stop being a guest and help. Contribute, and become important. Play a different role, and be a force.

Do not say you will bring a salad. Do not say you will sing a song. Do not say you will help. Any guest can do that. Help. Actively help. Do it, and you give. Do it, and you are great.

Zev Kahn loves his early morning trip to work – pale sun, rose sky, light breeze, swaying shrubs, clean air, chirping birds, traffic quiet.

But something about this precious time disturbed Zev. One early morning he realized what this was...

"I am making a mistake, " thought Zev, "The world is singing a song, but I am contributing nothing. Am I only a spectator? Only a guest?

"I can't let this happen," Zev decided, "I must also add to the beauty of the morning. I must enhance it. I must promote it. I must be a part of it!"

Just then, a young mail carrier cycled near him.

"YES!" Zev shouted at him.

"Yes...?" the mail carrier asked. His bicycle wobbled, stopped and he put a leg on the ground. He cocked his head towards Zev.

"Yes. This is a beautiful world, and today is a beautiful day," said Zev.

The mail carrier stared, then smiled.

"Have a good day yourself then," he said, as he wobbled away.

"And you have a good day too," called Zev at his departing back.

Part 2, in short...

(i) First do. First act. Then wait with hope for good things to happen. Look to that which is beautiful and powerful in the world, and become a part of it. See life as a glorious gift, and live it to the full.

(ii) Learn always more about the world, more about how it works. Thus, you will live life with more success and skill. Keep growing. Continue to create, to innovate. Do not rest on your laurels.

(iii) Adopt your world. Make efforts to enrich the lives of people around you. Give your mind and your strength to reach this goal.

(iv) Focus on giving. Even when you take, do so that you may give more. One who gives is great. One who takes is small.

(v) Life is a grand party. Focus on being one of the hosts – not one of the guests. Contribute in any way you can, and make the party a success.

PART THREE

You and Others

CHAPTER I

Give it to them

How do the greatest companies become great? How do they make those fabulous profits? They supply the market with great and fabulous goods. People buy what they want. The company who gives them their heart's desires, is the company that thrives.

At times, companies capture the market. They conquer and control it. This is because no one else is providing the products that people want. Other times they play tug-of-war with those who produce the same goods.

The secret of winning, of beating their competition, is to understand what people want of their product. They need to learn what they must provide, and how they can provide it.

Thus, if the market wants the product to be smaller and lighter, they must make it smaller and lighter. If the market wants it to be more powerful, sturdy, they must make it more powerful and sturdy. If the market wants it to be more elegant, more silken, they must make it more elegant and silken. If the market wants it to be cheaper, more convenient, they must make it cheaper and more convenient. What the market wants is what they provide.

This is the grand rule of business success. It is also the grand rule of being great.

All they need

All people interact with each other. They affect each other. Great people affect others more. They influence them. They change their lives. This is their greatness.

To affect other people's lives, you have to enter their lives; and to enter other people's lives, you need to win their respect. Whether you aim to influence the entire human race, your fellow citizens, your neighbors, or even simply, your own children, you must have their approval. You must gain their love and affection. You must earn their admiration. You must secure acceptance of who you are and what you stand for.

You do all this, when you give them what they want. Give them what they want, and they will come back to you. They will elevate you. They will support you. They will give you all you want.

No one could understand how Anton Elliot had moved up so quickly in the company. Certainly, he was skilled and able. The company however, had many skilled and able employees. Most of them had been with the company much longer than Anton Elliot.

Finally, someone asked Anton what his secret was. This is what he said:

"When my manager hired me, he told me what my job entailed – what were my duties, what were my responsibilities. Even at that stage, I realized that I had other tasks he had not told me about. One of these I knew, was to make sure he looked good next to the other managers. I also knew that this was especially important, when he stood with his seniors.

"When I did this, an amazing thing happened. My boss's bosses insisted on transferring me to their divisions. They saw how I praised my boss, and realized that I was the person they themselves needed. So, they promoted me to their divisions. This has already happened several times, and it seems that it will soon happen again.

"My trick is really no trick at all. It is obvious that every manager needs to impress his managers. If so, then his assistants need to assist him with this. I have only been carrying out my job, nothing more.

"The one thing I do not understand is why my fellow workers, all of them intelligent people, are not doing the same thing."

CHAPTER II

The secret

Give people what they want, and they will come back to you. They will elevate you. They will support you. They will give you all you want.

The question is then, what is it that other people want. What is it that you should give them?

There is only one answer to this question. This is that what people want, what they really need – once they have food and housing – is GREATNESS.

Supply the market with food and housing, survive your rivals who also supply food and housing, and you are in business. But, supply greatness, and the market is yours. Supply greatness and you have the greatest business of them all.

Make it your business to make others great.

> Excuse me friend, you're not making sense. First, you tell me I need to be great. That means that I have to be greater than others are. I have to stand out amongst them.
>
> Now, you tell me to make others great. What happens to me then? If everyone else becomes great, I lose my edge. I become another face in the crowd. How then am I supposed to be great?

The trap

'Make others great, and you make yourself small.' This idea is a giant obstacle to your greatness. 'Make others great, and you are nothing.' Because of this idea, many small people remain small. They hang onto this thought all their lives, and do nothing with their lives.

Worse still, they assume the opposite to be true. 'Make others small, and you make yourself great.' With this belief, they go to enormous lengths to belittle others, to nullify them. They strive to embarrass and destroy them. They toil even, to exterminate them. In doing this, they do a horrible harm to the world around them. Also, they cripple themselves.

They are wrong. They make a terrible mistake. Be careful! Do not fall for the same madness. Do not trip into the same trap.

You win, I win

The truth is that when you make more of others, you become more. To pull others up, you must be higher than them. In raising them then, you reach new heights. In enhancing and beautifying them, you become beautiful. In enlarging them, you become great.

Make others great, and you make yourself great. Applaud others, elevate them, glorify them, and you elevate yourself. Remember this, and use it. You need it.

The exciting moment had arrived. Andy Bookman had won the chemistry prize.

"Despite, or in spite of, my clumsy, incompetent staff," she thought wryly. It then occurred to Andy that she would have to make an acceptance speech.

"Should I thank those bungling fools?" she asked herself, "What is there to thank them for? They almost ruined the project not once or twice, but almost a dozen times...

"Should I then not thank them?" she asked herself.

Over the ten months they had worked together, Andy had made special efforts to befriend her four assistants. While they responded warmly to her affection, this did not affect the quality of their work. Andy had never before known such exasperation, frustration and agony.

At her acceptance speech, Andy did thank her staff. She could not, she felt, take all the glory for herself. Although they did not deserve it, she would share at least some of the honor with them. Andy looked long and hard to find good qualities in her assistants, and highlighted them in her speech. She praised them with tact, with generosity. Her staff was amazed and thrilled.

A short time later though, it was Andy's turn to feel surprise. A letter arrived offering Andy a prestigious appointment, a job she had only dreamed of receiving. One of the reasons, said the letter, for offering her this job, was the force of character Andy had shown in thanking her staff.

CHAPTER III

Not gratitude

Giving greatness to others leads to a greater greatness for you. Do not however, expect this to come in the form of gratitude. Moreover, try to not expect any short- term benefit from your kindness. If people thank you, accept their thanks graciously. Thank them for their thanks. If they do not thank you, forget it.

Do not worry when people are not grateful. You have given them something valuable, and they are in your debt. Sometime, in the near future, you will enjoy the delicious fruits of your good deed.

Small people

Small people do not know how to say thank you. Even when they were trained as children to say 'please' and 'thank you', their gestures are superficial ones. Their 'thank you' is a parrot's 'thank you'. They are locked in the jail of their own smallness, and cannot recognize a great act as being great. They are prisoners of their own perception. They cannot see beyond what they themselves are.

Therefore, they forget that is you who gave them their gift. They yank it; they snatch it – as though it was always theirs, as though you really owed it to them. Or, if they do recognize your kindness, they resent you for it. Somehow, they see your generosity as a way of mocking them, of taunting them. At times, they even respond with plain hatred.

Cal Spitz was stuck. He needed money, a lot of money, and seemingly, no one could help him.

Cal Spitz is a clever merchant running a brisk business. Right now though, he had cash flow problems. He had already obtained from the bank as much as they would give him, and he feared appealing to private lending agencies. Who could he turn to?

In desperation, he tried his rabbi.

"Sure Cal, take a seat and I'll see what I could do," said the rabbi, and he buzzed his secretary.

"Charlene," he told her, "we need to borrow some money; I want you to phone…" The rabbi started listing some of the wealthy men of the community as well as the sums he wanted from each one of them. Cal gasped at the sums, as well as at some of the names – they were his fiercest competitors.

"Wait in the outer office," the rabbi said to Cal, as he turned his head to his sacred studies, "the Lord will surely help us."

Forty minutes later the rabbi recalled Cal and presented him with the money.

"Thank you very much, Rabbi," said Cal, "I'll make sure you get the money back as soon as possible."

"One minute, Cal, take a seat. Here, have a cherry," said the rabbi pointing to a bowl of cherries that sat on his desk. Cal looked in surprise at the bowl, but did as he was told. The rabbi also ate a cherry.

"Have another one, Cal," the Rabbi told him, and did the same himself. In a short while, there was a neat heap of cherry-stones on the plate.

"Here Cal, take these stones, said the rabbi, "then, in the future if you have the urge to throw rocks at me, remember these cherry-stones, and use them instead.

CHAPTER IV

Feeling good

There are different types of greatness you can give others. You can help them 'feel great'. You can go into the entertainment business, and occupy their minds and hearts with your stories and songs. You can help them use up their hours, and make tremendous profits in the process.

When you do this, you help them relax. You relieve them of stress and tension. You even assist them to dream new dreams. Still, this does not make them great. And while you may gain some fame and fortune for yourself, these do not make you great either.

Looking good

Then, you can help people to 'look great'. The fashion and beauty industry is more powerful even than the entertainment business. Moreover, when people look good, their self-esteem rises. They accomplish more. When people look fine, they feel better too. They are happier.

Still, while beauty may invite approval, it will not satisfy you. While it may attract applause, it will not soothe you. Also, beauty does not match the reality of life. As you grow older, your beauty fades – naturally, it dies. How then can it be a goal when it keeps moving away from you?

A precious gift

The best greatness then, is to help people become great. This gives them much more than moments of distraction and pleasure, more even than possessing a glamour, a gloss, a skin-deep glory. This is something that is truly theirs; something no one can steal from them; something that will give them satisfaction and inner-peace; something that may even improve as they grow older and more senior. This is the most precious gift of all.

The problem is though, how do you give greatness to others? Surely, it is something they can only gain for themselves?

Raise them, boost them

You cannot make others great, but you can help them become great by themselves. You have tools to energize and strengthen them. The most powerful of these is encouragement.

All people during their every day have moments of greatness. They may do a piece of work in a neat, fresh way. They may spice a conversation with a perceptive, inspiring thought. They may show kindness to someone who has less than them.

These moments are all opportunities to help them climb the ladder of greatness. You need to catch the moment, and hold it up for applause. You need to light up and draw attention to its greatness. You need to endorse the deed, and praise it. You need to smile, celebrate and cheer their achievement. You need to make this moment a flash of glory.

Low high

Likewise, all people in their every day have their low periods. At such times, when they feel blue, when they feel that no one loves them, no one cares for them, they act small. They act mean. They indulge their lowest lusts – greed, conceit, jealousy. They disconnect themselves from society. They even engage in violence and crime.

This too is a chance to help them become great. Smile at them. Show them friendship. Draw them in. Ask them about their selves, their family, their interests, their goals, their lives. Be fascinated. Make them feel ten feet tall. Make them feel ten million dollars rich. Once they sense their own value, their own importance, they will act big, think big; they will be great.

You can give all this to them. All you need is to do it.

Penny was nine years old when Sherry Black adopted her. The first year was a nightmare.

Penny was introverted, unsociable, sullen. She was cruel, vicious, spiteful. She ignored those who approached her with friendship. She disregarded every family member, every teacher, every child. She refused to go to school or take lessons, and would kick and scream her rebellion. She gave her hours only to the rocking chair and her collection of shabby magazines. She would not wash herself or brush her teeth. She did not clean herself properly after the toilet.

Sherry hunted frantically for some way to connect with Penny. The best advice she heard was to catch Penny doing what was right. Catch her at it, and praise her for it.

Sherry followed this advice rigorously. She searched out Penny's every praiseworthy act, and cheered it with a full heart. To her amazement it worked. Penny thrived on the approval and admiration. At one point she was openly addicted to it, and went to great lengths to win Sherry's applause.

Gradually, Penny found her own beautiful self. She flowered into a sensitive, caring girl. She was neat and tidy. She helped in the house. She was principled in her schoolwork. She was affectionate, loving, and won the hearts of all who knew her.

"I gained all this," says Sherry, "this precious child, with Praise, Appreciation and Approval."

CHAPTER V

At the base

There is a tool that is more basic than encouragement. It is a tool that includes encouragement. It includes praise, appreciation, approval, and it includes more. This name of this important device is education.

> Encouragement is really a form of education? How do you work that out?

When you see others doing great acts, or speaking in great ways, and you compliment them for this, you educate them. When you encourage them, you tell them that you see what they do as being great. You show them the value that you attach to their behavior.

Moreover, when you praise and applaud others, you shift and alter their whole value system. For instance, before you praised them for being honest or thoughtful, they viewed this as having little weight. Now they see it as having a much larger value.

Conversely, when you object to what they do, when you show disapproval for what they say, you also educate them. You tell them that in your eyes they have done something small, something evil. You show them its ugliness, its deformity. And again you affect their perception. Again, you change their value system.

The challenge

The name 'teacher', is a bit of a wet cloth on a cold winter's day. It stirs an image of a colorless classroom, mumbling children, a critical instructor, dull lessons.

However, a 'teacher' is any person who changes the thinking of other people. In other words, any time you affect the point of view of others, you are their instructor. No matter how you sway their outlook, you are their educator. Thus, since all people touch all others in some way, they are all teachers.

You want to be great. Therefore, your challenge is to give greatness to others. Show them with skill, with firmness, how to be great. This is the key to your success. Learn how to be a competent educator.

Show them

People reach for greatness by creating for themselves goals, lofty goals, and following them. Only they can do this for themselves. In setting these goals however, they must rely on data that comes from beyond themselves, from outside of themselves – guidelines that come from the world around them.

The vision people strive to realize, the dream they want to develop, is made of elements they learn about. They cannot aim for a target that they cannot see. They cannot search for a destination they have never heard of. They must first receive an education.

Therefore you – who have lived through different experiences – need to show them new pictures, or new angles of old pictures. You need to acquaint them with different destinations, give them directions and point them towards greatness. You need to feed them with ideas and thoughts that they may include in their wish for the future. You need to paint a landscape of greatness before them, one that they can think about, that they can absorb, and that they can adopt. When you do this, you are a great educator.

Directions

When you see someone standing next to his car, staring in confusion at a street map, you go over to him, and help him. You offer him directions. If you see that he did not listen properly, if you see him starting off in the wrong direction, you call to him again and set him straight.

Similarly, when you see others have lost their path through life, you must try to set them straight. Try to direct them away from that which can harm them. Try to guide them towards that which is good.

Still, people who are bodily lost, are different to people who are inwardly lost. When you help others find a physical destination, you do not hesitate to approach them. Likewise, they feel no disgrace about making their error. But with people who are inwardly lost, you need to act with sensitivity, with subtlety. Otherwise, they will regard your good intentions as interference, as intrusion. Worse still, you may shame them. You may humiliate them.

All this makes it difficult to direct those who are truly lost. Nevertheless, it is possible. With a little thought, a little tact, a little humor, you can make a difference. It may cost you time and effort. Still, part of being great is giving of your time. Part of being great is making that extra effort.

Daryl Seer went to work at 16. At the age of 24, he made his first million. Since then, he has made many more. Still, despite his tremendous wealth, Daryl kept a low profile for many years. Then he changed his approach. This is how he explains it:

"I always admired the attribute of modesty. People who flash their wealth before others, remind me of monkeys at the zoo. They perform antics for peanuts. Also, I found that hiding my wealth helped me come closer to others, especially to my workers. It allowed me to be 'one of the boys'.

"Recently, I remade myself. I had my office decorated with expensive fittings. I switched my old sedan for a new sports car. I started wearing designer clothing. Why did I do this?

"I find the youth of today quite different to the youth of ten years ago. On the one hand, they are more intelligent, mature and insightful. They are more ready to live and let live.

"On the other hand however, they are pampered. They have a taste for the easy life. They are addicted to comfort, leisure and self-indulgence. They do not know how to work, or how to save up for that which they want. They do not know how to strive, to fight. They appreciate and crave the fruits of success, but they will not toil and persevere to reach them. This I think, is the reason we see so much unhappiness, so much corruption and even suicide amongst today's youth.

"My family, friends, employees, know me as a hard worker. They understand that I am determined, focused, forceful. However, they view all this as old-fashioned, prehistoric. I want to change this. I want to show them that it is through being 'prehistoric' that today I enjoy all the luxury items they so admire, they so desire. I want to teach them the value of my ways. I want them to learn from my example.

"More than this, I am arranging for someone to write my biography. I know that there are many books that tell the rags to riches' story, but I think a new work with a present- day hero, someone people know, may help revive the work ethic that brought me my success. If in some small way I can affect today's youth, I am ready to tolerate the absurdity of being 'stylish' and 'a playboy'."

CHAPTER VI

Not close, not far

Do not show people who are lost, something too far from them. They will not see it. They cannot connect with a picture they cannot see, with an idea they cannot hear. They will ignore it, and your effort will be wasted. You have to show them that which is only a little way beyond them – not too close, not too far.

That which is too close, they will shrug off. "That's too simple. I've heard it all before. What do you want from me?" they will demand with irritation. That which is too far, they will also shrug off. "That's not me; that can't be me," they will say.

Sometimes, the picture you paint must contain an obscurity, a mystique, a hint. To catch the attention of your listeners, they must feel it is something worth catching. Then they will exert themselves to hear and see it. Then they will open their hearts to the idea.

With heart, with love

'Words that come from the heart, enter the heart.' This is a key to effective education.

Give your heart to building others. Do it with sincerity, with attentiveness, with care. Focus on the person or people you want to help. Concentrate on enlarging them, on benefiting them. Wrap them with the mantle of your love.

You and I, one

There is a secret to giving to others, a secret to giving them your heart. There is a golden rule to loving others. This is to identify totally with them.

You need to see their welfare as your welfare, their prosperity as your prosperity. You need to look on their victory as your victory, their happiness as your happiness. You need to feel their greatness as your greatness. You need to suffer their pain as your pain.

To love others as you love yourself, you need to love the two of you as one.

Charles, Jack and Ivan Balfour are three brothers. They all became dentists.

"It is amazing," says Jack, "that three brothers who grew up together, played together, fought together, should choose the same profession."

"What is even more amazing," says Ivan, "is that today we work together in the same practice."

"Our lives are intertwined as never before," adds Charles. "Not one of us works simply for himself and his family – he works for all three of us. We have revived the famous call – 'One for all. All for one!'"

"I never really understood that phrase before," says Ivan, "now, I live it. The feeling is fantastic."

"I am more alive than ever before," adds Ivan, "I live for the three of us, I feel for the three of us, I strive for the three of us. Instead of being one person, I am three. I have tripled."

"There is a story," says Charles, "of a drunk who turns to his drinking partner and sobs, "if you were really my friend, you would tell me what hurts me." I really feel that as super-partners, we laugh together, we cry together."

"I know of husband-wives who are as apart as two strangers ever were," says Jack. "Now that I know what it is to have the opposite of this – both at home in my own marriage and here at work with my brothers – I really feel sad for them."

"Our challenge today is," concludes Jack, "to take this beautiful sense of unity that we have here, and extend it to the rest of our family, our patients, neighbors, friends and everyone else we know."

CHAPTER VII

Through and through

A sign that you have reached GREATNESS, is when you stop thinking only of yourself, your comfort, your gain, your future. Instead, you look after your greater body, the people around you, your street, your town, your world.

Therefore, do not think, "how can I improve my situation?" Think rather, "how can I improve our situation?"

Do not think, "what are my hopes for the future?" Think rather, "what are our hopes for the future?"

Do not think, "what are my targets?" Think rather, "what are our targets?"

Even when you are not actively involved with the lives of others, you can think in this way. You may place your wages in your own pocket, you may spend it on your own needs, but when you think, think of the greater community.

Do this, and you generate a sense of goodwill. Do this, and you produce harmony amongst many, many people – those you know, as well as those you may never meet.

A condition

The problem with the above idea though, is sincerity. It has to be real. To stop thinking 'I', and start thinking 'us', you must live it. You must be it. To hang onto such giant, vast, broad thoughts, you must in some way live them, concretize them. You must do something to solidify this approach. You must do something to maintain your noble intent. This something is GIVE.

A great philosopher once calculated that if everyone in the world gave 1% of his or her earnings to charity, there would be no more poverty. This is the power of giving.

Give

To reach for greatness you have to start not with the world, but with yourself. Decide now to become a giver. And back up this decision with a commitment, with a promise.

Resolve that from this point on, that you will give at least 10% of your earnings to those who have less than you. This is the famous biblical tithe. Very wealthy people today will point to this tithe and tell you that it is the secret of their good fortune.

Ten percent of your net earnings is not that large a sacrifice. It is also not so difficult to do this if you give it as soon as you receive it. The problem lies when you delay your promise. Your debt then grows huge. It becomes a mental mountain – one that looks invincible.

Ignore the debt, let it slide away and dissolve, and you lose it. For no one will come to your door and demand this money. No one will beg and plead with you for it. And so, you will lose the opportunity to help others. So, you will lose the greatness that comes from this act.

Time out

There is another tithe you can give. This is 10% of your time. There is much you can buy with money. There is also much that money cannot buy. There are many areas where only your participation, your physical contribution, makes a difference.

This does not have to be 10% of your total day, almost two and a half hours. It can be a tithe of the active, profitable, money-earning part of your day.

If you work an 8-hour day, this translates into 480 minutes. Make a resolution then to give at least 48 minutes each day to others, to those less fortunate than you. Give some of this tithe-time to your children. Give it also to family that is more distant. Give it to your neighbors. Give it to strangers. This is an important part of being great.

Janice Dancer has a general store. In it she sells pots, pans, socks, shirts, canned foods, cakes, candles, soaps, perfumes, sunglasses, toys, etc.

"If my shop were 6 stories high, I would have a department store," says Janice.

Still, Janice's store is a wonder. Its place is next to a modern shopping center that boasts many specialty shops as well as great department stores. All these glitter with artistic windows and chic lines. By rights, Janice's store should be dead, an anachronism, a quaint piece of history. Janice however, hires five assistants, and they are busy all day. What is the secret of her success?

Along with running the store, Janice has another business. She calls it 'a cup of tea'. In one corner of the store, Janice has tea, coffee, sugar, sweetener, milk, and a tub of fresh cookies. In the same corner also, is Janice herself. Here she makes herself available for all who come with their tales of woe and misery.

Janice listens with patience to the stories of others. She gives them her attention, her concentration. She even offers a little advice, though not too much. She allows her customers to talk as much as they want. There is no charge for this service.

Janice has made many friends with her store. She is often a guest at weddings, engagements and graduations. Sometimes, she also goes to funerals...

"My profits are smashing," says Janice. "The store is thriving. Still, my greatest gains are my personal ones. I derive huge satisfaction from all I do for others. Simply by listening, I show people how to feel good about themselves. Simply by caring, I help them turn misery into success, despair into laughter.

"Of all the people I have helped, I have helped myself the most. I am a different person today, wiser, more mature, more patient, more caring. I love being who I am."

Janice is a great woman.

Part 3, in short...

(i) To affect other people's lives, you have to enter their lives. To enter their lives, you must win their respect. To win their respect, you must give them what they want.

(ii) What people most need and want, is to be great. Therefore, make it your business to make others great. This is in turn, will make you even greater.

(iii) Usually those you give to are smaller than you are. Therefore, do not expect repayment or thanks from them. Know though that every great act you do produces fruit. This is a fruit you will enjoy.

(iv) You cannot actually make others great, but you can help them become great. The best tool for doing this is encouragement.

(v) Do not just encourage others. Educate them. Show them what it means to be great. Point them towards greatness.

(vi) Give your heart to building others. Care about them as you care for yourself. See their welfare as your welfare. View their prosperity as your prosperity.

(vii) Think thoughts that go beyond you – beyond your comfort, beyond your future, beyond your own gain. Think rather, of your greater self. Focus on your greater body. This body is the people around you, your street, your town, your world.

Back up this outlook by giving of yourself to others. Give at least 10% of your earnings to those who have less than you do. Give at least 10% of your time to those who need your help.

PART FOUR

You

CHAPTER I

To be

Doing great acts is not enough. You have to be a great person. Nevertheless, by doing great acts, you can become great. Every act you do, in some small way, affects your entire personality.

For instance, if you are harsh, demanding, intolerant, if you forever snap at others, you are an impatient person. Forcing yourself to act in an easygoing way will not change this. Your performance might win you an award, but it does not make you something you are not.

However, if you keep up this act, daily, for a long time, this will alter your character. If you train yourself to do this willingly, gladly, you will be a more serene, calm, patient person.

Alone

Great people do great things. But, even when they are not doing anything, even when they sit quietly, alone, they are great. Being great does not depend on what they do. It does not depend the opinion of other people. It does not depend on anything besides themselves.

You interact with the world around you. You take a shower. You drive your car. You do your work. You buy your groceries. You drink your coffee. You look at the clouds. You pick flowers. You jump over fences. If you lived in a world where there were no showers, cars, work to do, groceries, etc., none of this would be possible.

You interact with people. You talk with your husband or wife. You argue with a taxi driver. You give instructions to your secretary. You smile at a customer. You bother your bank manager. You play with your children. If you lived all alone in the world, none of this would be possible.

But besides the time you give to your world and the people who inhabit your world, you also spend time alone. You also spend time by yourself, not doing anything, not involved in anything. At such moments, you also need to be great.

Don't kill it

No matter how busy you are, no matter how big your burdens, how difficult your duties, no matter how many people you speak with and deal with, there are quiet moments in your every day. There are moments when you are alone with your thoughts, alone with yourself. Here too you need to be important, alive. Fill these moments with thoughts that are important, alive, and you are great. Kill these moments, and you kill some of yourself.

There are people who cannot bear to be by themselves. They cannot spend the shortest time in their own company. They must do something, handle something, say something. They must have music and noise and activity. They forever run away from themselves.

But they are wrong. They make a terrible mistake. All people must learn to be alone. They must enjoy being alone. If necessary, they must train themselves to be alone. This is vital for their health and happiness.

Simon Ruddy could not believe it. This was like the kids' storybooks, like the movies. Here he was, stuck on a big rock in the middle of the sea. He had a fresh-water pool. He had coconut trees. The weather was pleasant. And he was alone.

Simon had gone sailing early that morning, got lost in a storm, smashed his boat on some rocks, and was absolutely stranded. For how long? Who knows?

Simon has a sweet wife, two growing children, and two dogs. He owns a good business. He lives in a fine house. He rides horses. He cycles. He skis. He dives. He boats. Still, Simon is not happy. He openly admits this.

"What's eating you, Simon," a friend asks.

"Nothing really," he answers.

Being shipwrecked did not really worry Simon. "Someone is sure to come by," he thought. He was not too anxious about home or work either. His wife was efficient, levelheaded and would not panic. His secretary was used to running his business by herself.

"Maybe," thought Simon, "this will bring some adventure, some excitement, back into my life."

Simon spent almost two weeks on his island. Help did not come as quickly as he thought it would. It also was not exciting. No fierce savages or animals threatened him. There was no lack of food and drink. There were no vicious storms to weather.

Still, Simon spent the time in a way better than he ever would have imagined. For the first time in many years, Simon spent time alone. Simon got to know himself.

As Simon strode the beaches, he asked himself many probing questions:

"Am I a good husband? Do I fulfill my duty as a father? I send the kids to good schools and take care of all their material needs, but is this enough?

"A friend once hinted to me that I live only for myself – is this true? Am I only looking out for myself, or do I give to others as well?

"What is the purpose of my life? Where am I heading? Where will I be in ten years' time? Who will I be in ten years' time? In twenty years' time? Am I the person I would like to be? Do I like myself?

Simon returned from his 'vacation' with new solutions, with new resolutions. He had adjusted some of his perspectives, some of his priorities. He was more relaxed, positive, goal directed. He was ready to work. He was ready to change.

The new Simon surprised and delighted his family and friends. The new Simon enjoyed being the new Simon.

CHAPTER II

Respect

What are the qualities you need to take pleasure from yourself? The attributes that allow you to enjoy being alone, enjoy spending time with yourself? One of them is honor.

All people need others to respect them. A life where others think nothing of you, where they hate you, is no life. A life where others are cold, indifferent, unfriendly towards you, is dismal. It would be better to be dead than to live in such a way.

In contrast, the more others respect you, the more alive you are. The more they acknowledge and accept you, the more they admire, appreciate and befriend you, the more cheerful you are. And the ultimate expression of such respect, such honor, is love. This leads to an even greater happiness. How do you win such respect?

Devices

Children will draw pictures, sing songs, dance and pour cups of juice, to win a parent's approval. Like children, adults also seek and hunt the approval of others. They use a medley of tactics to win attention and admiration from all who know them. They even want total strangers to think highly of them.

One of these devices is to dress in stylish, sharp ways – to seek out clothes that play out, that promote their good looks, gems to decorate their bodies, paints to color their heads.

Another device is to buy costly extras – to live in grand homes, surround themselves with antique furnishings, unique fittings, drive high-priced cars, plug into high- flying gadgets, buy yachts, planes and helicopters, like kids buying candy.

Yet another device is to act in an attractive way – to listen wide-eyed and open-mouthed to other people's stories, giggle and flirt, tell jokes and fall on the floor laughing at others' jokes, flatter and stroke and backslap others.

These devices all work. They draw attention and admiration, even awe. There is a problem though. For they are a little like saltwater to the thirsty.

When you draw high regard in such ways, you feel keenly, that this high regard is not for you, but rather for your dress or your car or your performance. It is your appearance that draws admiration. It is your fortune that people praise. Very little of the approval is yours.

At every level

This problem is a problem not only when you buy honor 'cheaply'. It seems to exists at all levels.

Imagine. You are a politician who has fought your way to the top. Now, everywhere you go, reporters film and photograph you. They record and broadcast your every word. But, how much of this honor is for the position you hold, and how much of it is for you?

Imagine. You are a scientist who has worked for decades to find a new cure for an old virus. When you finally discover it, your popularity soars. The world covers you with awards and applause. But, how much of this glory is for your new drug, and how much of it is for you?

Imagine. You are an author who has sweated over a new class of work, who has broken into fresh fields of thought. Everywhere you go, your book is on display. Everyone wants to read it. They all welcome and salute your effort. But, how much of the importance belongs to your composition, and how much belongs to you?

Your works and you

The more you labor over a project, the more it becomes a part of you. When you invest time, effort, focus, concentration, sweat and tears into a specific mission, then it is you. When you sleep, eat and breathe it, then it is you. It is as much a part of you as an arm or a leg. As such, when your work receives praise, it is your praise. You may enjoy it in a full way.

On the other hand, when you receive something as a gift, with no effort at all, then it remains outside to you. It cannot be yours. It will not be yours. Likewise, the acclaim such a gift draws, is also not yours. Those who admire your physical beauty or your inherited wealth, are not admiring you. Their praise therefore, cannot satisfy your hunger for recognition and respect.

"I discourage my children from coming to my performances," says Noel Robyn, lead vocalist of a popular rock group. "I want them to know me as a real father – not the symbol the public sees.

"Don't get me wrong. I am proud of what I do on stage. I have trained and toiled to create my image. I take my work seriously because I know it is important...

"I show my audiences exuberance, a love of life. Through my example, they also come to express exuberance and a love of life. I sing with passion because life must be lived with passion. With this, I teach the world to live with passion. I sing of power, productive power, and I help my fans, my friends, to release the beautiful, fruitful, creative power that lies in each one of them.

"Still, the figure that appears on the stage is not the real me. My makeup artist paints a shimmering mask on my face. My dresser squeezes me into luminous suits and silver slippers. I prance rather than dance. I bellow rather than speak. I scream rather than sing.

"So when the crowds howl their approval, when they applaud and adore me, when they roar out my name, it is not actually me they turn to...

"I would like my children to know the real me ... no, that isn't true ... I hunger for my children to know the real me. I ache for them to know a warm, human father – one who helps them with schoolwork and shares their jokes, who kisses away their bruises and plays ball, who cooks breakfast and tucks them into bed, who knows them and holds them and loves them.

"And I need my children to love me..."

CHAPTER III

Superstars

It is however possible for you to gain a real respect – to know the acceptance and esteem of your true self. You can merit that others admire more than just your fine eyes, your comical stories, your cash flow, your exploits.

All this starts when you learn and train yourself to recognize and respect others.

All people who breathe, move, live on this earth believe that they are better than others are. Not only are they better than some others are, they are better than every other being in the world. They feel they have a unique quality, a matchless talent, a rare greatness, that no one else shares.

Are they right? Yes, they are. Just as no two people in the world have the same face, so too no two people have the same personality. Each one is special. Each one has a special quality, a special strength. Each one has a special treasure that is his or hers, and nobody else's.

The whole world is splendid, brilliant in its design, in its detail. Likewise, all people in the world are splendid, brilliant in their design, in their detail. With their beautiful bodies, their wide network of emotions, their complex, yielding brains, they glow like suns, like stars. They are a slice of a universe that is the final work of art, the puzzle of puzzles, the secret of secrets. As such, they too reflect this excellence.

Your Judge

You need others to respect you. You need them to honor you. This means that every time you meet someone, you ask them to think highly of you. You ask them to judge you generously, kindly. You know that people you meet automatically rank you, instinctively they assess you. You want them to decide in your favor.

They are your judges. They are your courtroom. You want to make the right impression. How do you do it? Listen carefully then to the way they think:

"Hmmm, you want us to greet you? You want us to respect you? You want us to think highly of you?

"Let's see. First, we need to know, are you intelligent or not. The sign of such intelligence is how you greet us, how you view us, how you respect us. If you know how to appreciate us, then all is well. If not, you must be stupid. Surely, you do not expect us to recognize and respect a stupid person?"

You want others to see greatness in you? Then you must see it in them. You want others to respect you? Then you must respect them. You want others to admire you? Then you must admire them. You want others to love you? Then you must love them.

Think it

To respect others means that you greet them, ask after them, ask after their families. It means you smile at them, encourage them, support them. It means you take an interest in their interests, you listen to their talk. It means you share their sorrows, and what is still harder, you share their joys. It means you wish them well, you wish them success – with all your heart.

The basis of this respect is to think highly of others. And for this to happen, you need to look at them as being more important than you are.

More than you

When others have more than you do, when they are richer or wiser than you are, it is easy to think of them highly. You however, need to see all people as being greater than you are – that is, even when they are smaller than you are. How?

The trick is to think like this: "Since they grew up with fewer skills, assets and opportunities than I did, clearly they cannot match me…

"But, when I subtract from my achievements the many gifts I have received all my life, I will see suddenly that my deeds shrink.

"Also, when I add to their few good deeds the weight of all the setbacks and sorrows they suffered during their lives, the value of their deeds jumps dramatically."

Look at them this way then, and see that their smallness well outweighs your greatness.

You them, them you

To appreciate others, all others, is itself a trait worthy of praise. The rule is that as you appreciate others, they in turn appreciate you.

It might appear that this rule does not always work. But if you study each situation carefully, you will see that it is a powerful, consistent rule. Sometimes people complain, "I was so nice to him – look how he repaid me!" Still, if they look carefully at what happened, they will see that their 'niceness' was not so very nice. They will see that they really were paid back measure for measure.

All for you

When you appreciate others, they appreciate you – and you appreciate you! Respect others, or better still, respect the entire world. Thus, you will find one of the greatest qualities of all, self-respect.

Love others. Love your world. This will fill your thoughts, and your entire self, with love.

Love others, and they will love you. Love your world, and it will love you. You will then live in a world of love.

Lynn Pert has bittersweet memories of her schooldays. While she tasted some triumphs, her heart still aches for the loneliness and isolation of those days. Her big regret was and is, how she failed to befriend her classmates.

At school Lynn had hungered to be a member of 'the gang', one of the girls. She tagged along after the others, but somehow it never helped. They simply closed her out. She never heard the joke or bit of gossip being repeated. She never joined in one of the games. She never shared a fruit or cookie from another girl's lunch-box. She even persuaded Mom not to make her birthday parties – she was ashamed that Mom might see that she had no friends.

Lynn tried as a child to figure out why she was rejected. Was it because she was ugly? Mom often told her that she was pretty. Was it because she was no good at sports? Ruthie didn't play sports and she had plenty of friends. Was it because she was top of her class? Surely, there is nothing wrong with that!

As an adult, Lynn feels she has worked it out. The barrier that existed between her and the other girls was of her own making. Somehow, she had viewed her classmates as being inferior to herself. Mom had also promoted such feelings. Together with her natural shyness, the result was disastrous.

Still, Lynn believes that this wretched period of her life forced her to acquire her most valuable asset. Her isolation drove her to examine the workings of human friendship. Lynn learned the secret of regarding other people as being important and special, and letting them know that they were important and special.

Now, Lynn's social skills outclass all those who 'naturally' know how to win friends and keep them. In the law firm where Lynn works, she is regarded as a top negotiator. Her services are sought out for the most sensitive meetings.

But what is especially precious to Lynn is that she has befriended almost every person in her life, from the moody janitor who takes care of her apartment block, to her nervous, highly-strung boss. The frustrating, stressful scenes that plague her colleagues, just never happen to Lynn. One and all, people smile at her, wave to her and are happy to see her. They respect, admire and love her.

CHAPTER IV

No complaints

Another mark of greatness is being able to anticipate reality. This means that you know that life sometimes gets tough, sometimes gets harsh. Therefore, when the unexpected creeps up on you, you do not panic. You deal with the problem calmly, firmly.

Being able to see reality also means that you do not fall apart when others let you down, when life lets you down. You appreciate that black is black. You know that white is white. Therefore, you do not tear our your hair when black does not turn into white. You do not fall apart when white does not turn out black. You did not expect a miracle. So, when it does not happen, you do not complain.

Many gifts

Most children as they enter the world, receive many gifts. They have fully functioning bodies, eyes that see, ears that hear, arms and legs. They have breathing systems, digestive systems, blood-dispersal systems, nervous systems, intelligence, etc. They have parents who feed them, clean them and care for them.

As they grow, they receive more gifts. Their parents continue to supply their material needs, food, clothing, shelter, and medical care. They also supply them with their emotional and intellectual needs; they teach and train them, they speak to them, they play with them, they hug, kiss and love them.

Also, they begin to receive society's gifts, streets and parks, schools and public libraries, shopping facilities. Other adults enter their lives. They find new friends to play with, to grow with. The world turns around them; it shows them its different aspects, startling faces, new things to excite them, to challenge them, to enchant and hypnotize them. The list of gifts they receive is a long one.

The nature of such gifts however is that they never fully belong to a person. In a second, they may be stripped of them, one or all. They may mislay a coin; they may lose their homes. They may quarrel with their friends; they may lose their families. They may catch a cold; they may lose their power of speech. They may sprain their ankle; they may drop dead.

Don't stop

Being realistic means enjoying the gifts you receive. It means using, consuming and relishing them to the full. After all, you possess them. You control them. So, don't hold back.

Moreover, being realistic means you make plans for your future. You have a set of expectations. With these in mind, you make provisions. You prepare. You expect that the health you have today, the cash coming into your bank account, the purr of your motorcar, will still be with you next week, next month, next year. And so, you plan a holiday at the seaside, a new paint-job for your house, a wedding spread for your child. You expect a bright future, and you save money for a bright future.

However, being realistic also means that if your car fails, your finances sink, or even your health slides – as they may all do – you will not fall. You will not disintegrate. You will not break down. You will continue to live and love and laugh.

Happy to be alive

Being great means enjoying what you have.

Give one child an expensive toy. In five minutes he drops it in a dusty corner. Give another child an empty milk carton. He plays with it for hours.

A strapping young man joined a picnic in the mountains. The scenery was stunning. The weather was heavenly. The food hamper was luscious. The company was lively. But he was annoyed and angry, and he sulked the whole day, because the wine was not chilled.

Then there is the sickly, old woman sitting in the garden of a shabby home for the aged. She has lost her dear husband. Her family never comes to visit. She is physically weak and suffers from pain. Her sight is almost gone, as is her hearing. Still, she breathes in the fresh morning air, and smiles. She thanks the Lord that she is alive.

Mark Glass is married to his favorite friend. He has two charming daughters. He lives in an average house in an average neighborhood. He works a 9 – 5 job, and now and then, overtime. He has average chores to do, get the lawn mowed, take the girls to art classes or the dentist, service the car. He has the average problems, repair a burst pipe, fill in for a sick co-worker, fill out income-tax returns. He has the average duties to perform, visit the children's school, vote in the local elections, take out the garbage. He has the average pleasures, an evening out with his wife, a holiday, a birthday party.

Still, there is something special about Mark Glass. He is one of the happiest people you will ever meet.

Mark makes it a point every morning, to meditate on all the wonderful blessings he enjoys, the sun that shines, the cock that crows; his ability to open his eyes, sit up in bed, stand, walk, do. He lets gratitude wash over him that he is clever and strong, that he can hear and speak, that he has a home, clothes to wear, furniture, appliances. He rejoices that he can wish his lovely wife 'good morning', cuddle his kids, and that he has an interesting, challenging day ahead of him...

Mark makes a point of tasting the food he eats, not only the first spoonful, but every spoonful. He appreciates the food, and his ability to eat it. As he steps out of his house, Marks takes a deep breath of fresh air in praise of the day. Mark will often say, even to complete strangers, isn't today just wonderful...

Mark trains his thoughts on the gift of being alive. He draws the attention of his family and friends towards all that is splendid, magnificent, harmonious about the world. He sings thanks not only with his lips, but with his heart. Mark celebrates life.

CHAPTER V

Better than a gift

You gain all that you have, all that you need, in one of two ways. You either work for it, or you receive it as a gift. That which you receive as a gift, you do not need to work for – you already have it. That which you do not receive as a gift, you must either wait until it lands in your lap, or you must strive and toil to obtain it.

Usually, an item you make for yourself is worth more to you than one you receive. Thus, a house you build is dearer than a house you buy; a table you construct is more precious than one you inherit; a meal you cook is tastier than one you eat in a restaurant.

This does not mean that you need to prepare every cup of coffee you drink. There is a value and pleasure in having others assist you, having them serve you. Still, you should not depend on the services of others. If there is no one to cater to you, cater for yourself. If there is no one to help you, help yourself. Be independent.

Free yourself of leaning on others. Although they are your employees, your servants, you may still end up depending on them, being a slave to them.

Similarly, do not rely on the gifts of others. You may have people who support you – pay for your room, board, tuition, buy your clothing and books. Still, know that you do not depend on them. Know that you can survive without them. In almost every situation, it is possible to live without gifts.

Create your own happiness

What makes you happy? It is accomplishing. It is achieving. These activities have a great happiness factor built into them. According to the pain, is the profit. According to the exertion, is the pleasure.

Do not look for others to entertain you, to fill your hours. Fix your own targets, and reach for them. Set your own goals, and pursue them. Construct your own dreams, and follow them. Your happiness depends on you.

That which you make yourself, is truly yours. Your plan, your plotting, your maneuvering, your negotiating, make it all yours. Your effort, your toil, your blood, sweat and tears, make it all yours. According to your pain, is your profit. According to your agony, is your ecstasy.

For twenty-two years, Nancy Margot lived as a complacent married woman. Her world was her thriving lawyer husband, her growing son and daughter, and her stylish home. Then, just as her children were reaching adulthood, her son off to college, her daughter working and affianced, her husband decided he too wanted a change. He left Nancy for his secretary.

This blow was a heavy one. Nancy had worked hard to be a fine wife, a compassionate mother, an efficient homemaker and host. She felt entitled to the comfortable house, the flow of money, the company of her amusing husband and lively children. They were a part of her soul, a part of her body. She had assumed that they would always be there. Now she had nothing.

Nancy had to trade her easy life for a small apartment, a small income, and a small, lonely self.

Her first few years were dreadful. She needed so much – she needed money, she needed people, she needed a new role to play. Yet, the horizon remained bleak.

No one called her, and when she called them... her ex-husband's line was busy; her children sent warm regards, but were busy, her few friends sent cards of sympathy and flowers, but were also busy. She could find no suitable work – she was too respectable, too untrained, and too old for the jobs on the books.

Nancy came close to breaking down. However, the shock of her fall, served to wake her up.

"No one else may need me," she declared, "but I need me. And I will help me."

Nancy redid her attitude, and redid her life. She took herself firmly by the hand, and created a new Nancy. She cheered up her apartment. She opened a small business. She built a new circle of friends, a 'family' that she could boost and encourage.

Soon Nancy was a cheerful, smiling, energetic, consolidated force. She was busy, very busy. Everyone needed her, her new friends, her old friends, her children, and even her ex-husband. They had all been too busy for the old Nancy, but they loved the new one.

Looking over her last few years, Nancy says that it took a landslide to move her. "While I very much wish to remarry, still I adore being the person I now am. I feel strong, vital, and healthy. It's a pleasure to be alive."

CHAPTER VI

The fire inside

A fire burns within you. It gives you energy. It warms you. It serves as a light.

Daily, you take care of this fire. You feed it, fuel it. You clear it, clean it of the waste, the materials that will not burn, the food your body cannot use.

Agitation, panic, fear, are not good for your fire. They dampen and pour cold water over it. On the other hand, when you feel excited, inspired, bright, happy, the fire blazes. It glows.

Control

A fire however, also needs supervision. It needs control. It must be nurtured, encouraged, cared for. But it almost must be contained, tamed. The worst danger is the fire that flares up and rages. It can burn all, destroy all.

Arrogance and cruelty, jealousy and anger, hostility and hatred – all these negative traits are fires out of control, fires that damage. While small, the injury they inflict is small. Their scarring is barely noticeable. Still, the nature of a fire is that it grows, it rages. And when it grows, its damage is great. It destroys. It kills.

In error

How do such negative traits, such sicknesses, penetrate the human mind? Their foothold is secured when people lose sight of reality. Their strength is born when they forget who they are and where they are.

Arrogance is the fruit of people who believe they are superior to others. This, they think, gives them the right to speak down at others, to humiliate them, to hurt them.

Cruelty is an extension of this arrogance.

> "Since I am better than them, I can order them around, I can torment them, I can torture them. I can do whatever I want."

But arrogant, cruel people make a mistake. They blunder terribly, and bring suffering and pain to others, and at the end, even to themselves...

"How do you, Mr. Arrogance, Ms. Cruelty, think you are better than others? Are you richer? Are you mightier? Are these the only qualities that count in life?

"Even if you are superior in one aspect, are you not inferior in several more? And even if you are 'all superior', does this give you license to pester others, to vex them? Does it permit you to cut into them, to scar them, to cripple them? Isn't such conduct itself a sign of inferiority?"

Jealousy and anger are also born as a result of poor thinking, poor understanding.

"If someone has something you don't have, Ms. Jealousy, something you cannot have, something you cannot afford, is the world then sick? Is justice then warped? Is this a reason to seethe, to fume, to snap at others?

"If all your expectations are not met, Mr. Anger, does this allow you to snarl, to scream, to howl, to burst? Do you deserve to have your every expectation satisfied? Are you sure you even deserve to be alive in five minutes time?"

Likewise, hostility and hatred are potent poisons. They burn inside people, and damage their health. They seek out and aggravate their natural weaknesses. They cause suffering and pain, and rob people of their strength. They provoke, and may even promote, major disease and death.*

These twin evils, hostility and hatred, also come from a failure to grasp life's realities.

"Why do you antagonize them, Mr. Hostility? Why do you scorn and despise them, Ms. Hatred? You say they hurt you? Are you sure they hurt you? Why would they hurt you?

"And you? Did you do nothing, say nothing at all to them? Are there no lapses here, no mistakes?

---

* Medical researchers have spent many years examining anger, hostility, depression and other negative emotions, and the way in which they affect hypertension, cardiovascular disease and other forms of illness. Their studies are not complete, but much of their data points to the damage these traits cause.

"Maybe they are mentally unbalanced? Maybe they are emotional cripples? Maybe instead of cursing them, you should feel sorry for them?"

Speak softly

A powerful device for controlling the fire inside is to wait – wait before you talk, wait before you answer those who annoy you. Then, when you do speak, speak quietly.

Do not react to a hot situation. Give the cool of your logic a chance to extinguish some of the passion. Then, when you respond, if you must respond, do it softly. This further gives your mind time to curb the spreading flames.

The resolution of one who is great, is to talk calmly to all persons, in all places, and at all times.

Cassy Burns is a clever, artistic woman. She also has a horrible temper.

Cassy is married to Brian, an ineffectual, spent man. He was quite a catch when Cassy married him, polite, pleasant, princely. They got on well together those first years. Cassy liked making decisions, and Brian was easy enough to accept them.

The problems began when Brian somehow did not live up to Cassy's expectations. Despite her love for Brian, Cassy could not resist now and then from complaining about Brian's shortfalls. Still, she was young and affectionate, and she guarded her tongue. Cassy and Brian had three children.

Later though, Cassy became less tolerant. She was less patient. She urgently needed to fix all that was wrong in the family, in the house. This need burned brighter every day.

"Why can't Brian and the kids do the chores I give them?" Cassy protested. "Can't Brian be more careful when he washes the dishes? Can't the kids keep the bathroom clean? Can't they pick up their clothes?"

Cassy became louder and uglier in expressing her rage, and Brian withdrew. He stepped back into his books, into his silence, into his coolness and apathy. He lost interest in the house, in his job, and in Cassy. Cassy became the main breadwinner.

While Cassy's bond with the children retained a 'normal look', she afflicted damage here also. The children treated her criticisms warily.

They followed her suggestions with obedience, but without cheer or joy. They hid their thoughts from her. They also hid their love from her.

Today, the family is still together. Only it is a sad house. Friends have tried speaking to Cassy, but she is quite deaf to their words. "Sure, I have a temper," she admits, "but it's the only way I can run things. If I didn't raise my voice, if I didn't threaten Brian and the kids with no supper or spending money, nothing would ever get done.

CHAPTER VII

A powerhouse

A fire burns within you. It gives you energy. It warms you. It serves as a light. Use this fire properly, and it will energize you, motivate you, empower you.

A fire burns within you. Use it creatively, constructively. With it, you can propel yourself and others to new heights, to new levels of achievement.

A steam engine is little more than a pot of water boiling on a stove. Yet, it is an amazing source of power. Years ago, it would move the massive trains. Today it powers the most advanced jet planes. With a thin burst of its steam, it torpedoes thousands of pounds of steel and cargo, into the heavens – all this is at supersonic speeds and within seconds.

Take care not to release your steam in the wrong way. In every situation, there are irritants, pests that annoy you, that trouble you. Know that these pests also serve you. They prod you. They prick you. They stir you from your complacency. They stop you from being smug.

That which irritates you is a gift. It ensures that you do not relax too long. It pushes you to keep climbing, advancing, doing. If however, you become angry, you spoil this gift. If you blow your stack, you fail this moment.

Build up

Sometimes the steam within you builds up into something you can no longer contain. It threatens to explode. At such times you must open a valve, an outlet, and release this steam.

The best outlet to discharge extra steam, is a creative one. You have no such an outlet ready? So, create one. Think of a home-repair you have been pushing off the last few months, and use this steam to fix it. Or, get out your running shoes and take a run. Look for a useful way to burn up your excess energy.

keep them burning

To feed your fires, to keep them blazing, you need to maintain them. Therefore, it is important to have a balanced mix of diet, exercise and rest. Too much food, even the healthiest type, chokes the fires. A lack of physical effort or an overload of physical effort also weakens the flame. Too much rest leads to sluggishness. Too little rest, over a long time, inflicts lasting damage.

Besides the physical food you provide your fires, you need its non-physical counterpart. These are items such as challenge, competition, excitement, stimulation. They also enhance the tone and gleam of the fire inside.

Anticipation

A special tool for maintaining your fire is anticipation.

See the young woman before her wedding day. She thinks about her fine gown and her cheeks glow. She imagines her new home and her eyes sparkle. She pictures the fun she will have, and her laugh is merry. She hums her wedding-song, and when no one is looking, skips and hops.

Her excitement over the coming event awakens some of her finest personal traits. She flowers. She is a butterfly. Her expectation of the event gives a special flavor and a thrill to the present moment.

Have something special to anticipate. Arrange a special event once a week. Plan on something bigger every few months. Set up something still bigger once or twice a year. Wait for an outing, a holiday, a reunion. Anticipate a special milestone. Have goals whose end you can hope for – passing a study course, completing a special project, winning a sports event.

After death

One problem with using 'anticipation' is what do you anticipate once you pass all your milestones. What awaits you after retirement? What is there to look forward to when you see your body declining, wrinkling, approaching death?

The answer is that you may – if you wish – think about life after death. This is surely something to anticipate. Also, this thought pushes you towards greatness. It tells you: "Prepare for this other life. Your material wealth has little worth in other worlds, so give more attention to your intangible riches. Refine your personality. Polish your traits."

You may not know that there is a life after death. On the other hand, you do not know that there is no life after death either.

What you do know is that one part of you, your physical body dies. Still, there is another part to you. It is your personality, your intellect, your emotions. It includes your sense of humor, your passion for life, your love of all that is beautiful. It also includes millions of memories. All this is non-physical. It is made up of some airy element that no scientist can grasp, no chemist can formulate. Could it be that this live on?

When you transfer a software program from one computer to the next, there is no change to the physical condition of either computer. Although you have moved the entire 'personality' from the first computer to the second, you do not affect its physical state.

It could be that at death, your personality – like that software – survives your body. It steps out of your dead flesh, and enters another world.

Cooking

Looking forward to a special event stokes your fire. In a like manner, so do other types of thoughts. Take an idea, something that fascinates you, something close to your heart, and meditate on it. Or, research and read about this topic, and think about it. Then, think about it again.

Do this, and you will find a stream of ideas entering your head. A landslide of thoughts will rattle your system. Your imagination will begin to race. Your heart will beat faster. Your whole self will start to cook.

You have the power to release such a force in you, and rocket yourself towards your highest ambitions.

Alan Knights is a fast-moving executive in a fast-moving company. He is respected and admired as being a 'powerhouse'. He states his ideas forcefully, and moves the whole labor force to follow him with eagerness. Furthermore, his ideas work. His bosses view him as their golden boy.

Where does Alan get this strength?

"I close my office door," says Alan, "sit at my desk, rest my hands over my eyes, and think. I pick a certain target, and think it through. Let's say for example, I wish to promote a new product. I sit still and let a picture of this product revolve in my mind. That's all.

"Gradually my body calms down, and different ideas start entering my mind. I don't jump on any ideas. I don't even write them down. I just let them flow through, at their own will.

"Later in the day, I repeat this exercise. Or, while driving through the streets, I will say the product name, and let any ideas I have, both old and new, roll around in my head. At night, I sleep on them.

"A day or so later, I am ready to form my plan. I arrange the most appealing ideas in an order of action. As I arrange them, I discard some thoughts and adopt others. When I do this, many new thoughts arise.

"Then, I run my plan through my head. I replay it immediately, and several more times during the week, adjusting it each time. This is the most exciting stage of all. Sometimes I become so fired, I literally jump and down. I pace the room like a lunatic. Still later, when I calm down, I am ready to sell my plan to others...

"I use this method not only for business. I use it for plotting family matters, home renovations, community concerns. It is a very powerful tool...

"I have done well in business, and I feel I will be ready soon to move into government. Several people have already approached me, but I am waiting for the right moment. My thought process will tell me when the time is right."

CHAPTER VIII

The golden cord

There is a thread, a golden cord of GREATNESS, running through the world. It runs through all places, at all times. It winds its way through all living creatures, all objects, all activities. Great people look always to see this thread. As much as they can, they keep in touch with it. They grip it. They hold tightly to it.

All that you do, you do either with greatness, or without greatness. All that you say, you say either with greatness, or without greatness. All that you think, you think either with greatness, or without greatness. It is all up to you.

Find it

To find GREATNESS, you must hunt for it, search for it. You must learn and grasp it.

You work in a large company. In exchange, your boss pays you a wage. This is the deal. Your share is to put in the time. The company's share is to give you the tools and pay your salary. Look to be great – do your share in a great way.

Find ways to give the company more for their money. Think how you can do your work more fully, more efficiently. Work to create a better product. Add to the enthusiasm and good cheer of your workplace.

The company will gain from such greatness, but you will gain more. You will profit in ways you never knew existed.

You manage a store. The store's objective is to sell the largest amount of goods and services. Strive to make the store a greater business than it is already. Study techniques to present your lines in more appealing ways. Know the selling power of the goods – which products should be on the shelves, and which products should be off them.

Look for ways to give your customers better service, ways to save them time and effort. Make your customers feel good about themselves. Make them feel great about buying in your store. Learn your business. Turn it, and yourself, into gold.

Mamas, Papas

You are a wife, a mother, a house manager. Your aim is to make a happy, healthy atmosphere at home. You provide your husband with his castle, that he may rule his roost, that he may love his home. You work cheerfully to build a dream house. You give your children love and warmth. You want them to enjoy childhood. You train them to be sensible, sympathetic and supportive of others. You urge them to grow into reliable, competent members of society.

Read material that will help you. Educate yourself to do a better job – even better than the one you do right now. Search out other women – women whose challenges match yours. Speak to them. Research different approaches. Enhance your home.

You are a husband and father returning from a day at the office. All you want is to pull off your jacket-tie, flop into an armchair and let go. But you know that when you reach home, other duties await you. The telephone rings. Your neighbor wants a few minutes. Your wife needs to discuss her day. Your children also want to be with, speak with and play with Daddy.

Plan a strategy to satisfy all sides in the best possible way. Think through your options. Run tests. Make the moments after you arrive home, moments of greatness.

And everything else

You need to change your diet. You have been feeling weak, sleeping badly. You are overweight or underweight. Your objective is a program that will give you maximum strength and energy, help you feel and look good, without disturbing your already busy schedule.

Make time to study different options. Read articles. Speak with the experts. Talk even with those who are not so expert. Look for people who are reaching the goals you wish to reach. Listen to their opinions. Then sift through the information. Accept and reject. Experiment. Learn and keep learning. Find that golden thread of greatness, and hold onto it.

You are adding a room to your house, you are investing money, you are planning a holiday, you have the day off. Prepare. Research and prepare. Listen to advice and prepare. Think and prepare. Plan, plan again, and prepare. Make your every move an important one, a beneficial one, a great one.

Adjust

Even when you hit on a successful approach, when you find the method and technique, look to improve it. Adjust it. Realign it.

Times change. Fashions change. Technology changes. Most important of all, you change. You are wiser than you were yesterday, or last week. You have gained knowledge, experience, practice. You are now a different person. So, do what you do in a different way. The way you always did it may be good, but now you have new skills, new strengths. Change your approach and do a better job. Do it now.

Moss Carp is an adventurer, an explorer. There is nothing new that she will not try, she will not examine. She even puts things in her mouth, just to see how they taste.

When Moss joins a conversation, she listens intently to all sides. She concentrates on their words. She seeks whatever she can gain from the moment. However, once the discussion becomes monotonous, boring, she moves on.

Moss looks always for new ways to do old things. She searches out new inventions, devices, oddities, and registers their features in the computer of her mind. She is certain that she will make good use of this information some time in the future.

Moss lives life with energy. She lives with enthusiasm and joy. Her every moment is precious to her, and she fills it to the brim. Is this because Moss is only two years old? Or, is it although Moss is only two years old?

A LAST WORD

Society

Search out other great people. If possible, try to create a group of great people, or even a world of great people. Start with the people around, a friend or two, members of the family, your children.

Still, the best way to create such a group is to start with you. Be an example, a role model. Let others see you happy, fulfilled, succeeding, growing and enjoying your life. Then make room for them to follow you. Encourage them to invent, to create. Stimulate them to do something new, and credit them for it. Let them teach you how to be great.

Role model

You, and every person in the world, needs to be great. You need it as you need food and shelter, family and friends. You do not wait for hunger pangs to attack before you shop for food. Similarly, do not wait for the need to be great to plague you, to haunt you. Seek out greatness now. Search for it with energy, with resolve, with focused thought. Make it your first priority.

Search for role models, and make them your model. Learn what greatness means, picture what greatness means, and pursue it. Your life is in your hands. Pattern it after that which is important, noble, exalted, admirable. Pattern it after that which is great.

He is old now, but he still has his liveliness, his spark. His knowledge is vast. His wealth is huge. He is also famous for his good sense, wisdom, kindness and humor. While he spends his days at home now, he still works for the good of society and the community.

She is his "other half" – a wife, friend, partner. She too is famous for her good sense, wisdom, kindness and humor. They have spent many years together. They suffered their hard times together. They celebrated their triumphs and joys together.

People gather in his living room each day. They wait for him. They want to speak with him, even for a few minutes. They come from government, the business community, schools, charities, and as private men and women. They come with their problems and worries. They leave with his advice, his blessing, his encouragement.

She is mother, grandmother and great-grandmother to a large, cheerful family. There is always at least one small child hanging onto the seam of her dress. But she also has time for her 'larger family'. She offers those who arrive, a piece of cake, a cold drink, a friendly smile. And they come away from their visit, with her advice, her blessing, her encouragement.

The visitor who enters his study, sees a comforting face. There is strength, calm, sense of purpose here. The visitor asks a question, and looks to a thoughtful expression. He sees in his eyes the desire to help, to support. The answer the visitor receives is short, to the point. Later the visitor will think the answer through more carefully, and understand it more deeply. The visitor thanks him, inclines his head with respect, and leaves.

The visitor who joins her on the couch, sees a comforting face. There is strength, calm, sense of purpose here. The visitor asks a question, and looks to the thoughtful expression. There is a strong desire here to help, to support. The answer the visitor receives is warm, but short and to the point. Later the visitor will think through the answer more carefully, and understand it more deeply. The visitor thanks her with respect, and receives a warm smile.

Their lives are quieter now than in earlier years. There is a serenity, a solidity, to their home. Still the needs and distress of people around them enter their lives and keep them both busy. They continue to give of their experience, compassion and wealth to others. Even so, they live with beauty and joy.

Who are these people? If you wish, they can be you.

Part 4, in short...

(i) Be great even when you are alone. Learn how to enjoy the time you spend by yourself. Learn how to use these moments in an important way.

(ii) You need others to respect and honor you. Approval you receive cheaply will not satisfy this need. But the praise you win with toil, sweat and tears, is a praise you will enjoy.

(iii) Others will recognize you when you recognize them. Others will respect you when you respect them. The basis of this respect is to look at them as being more important than you are.

Love others, and they will love you. Love your world, and it will love you. Thus, you will live in a world of love.

(iv) At times, life is hard, harsh. Expect this. Then, when it happens, do not panic. Plan a bright future for yourself. Still, when things do not turn out as you think they should, do not fall apart. Use all that life gives you in the best way you can. Strive to enjoy every moment of your life. Delight in the beauty of the world around you.

(v) Do not depend on others for your happiness. Know that what you make for yourself is worth more than what you receive. Therefore, make your own life. Take charge of your own happiness.

(vi) The fire that burns within you gives you energy. But you must restrain it. Do not allow it to flame into arrogance and cruelty. Do not let it flare as jealousy and anger. Do not let it rage as hostility and hatred. These are forces that will destroy you, as well as others. Speak softly at all times. This will help you control your fire.

(vii) Handle your fire properly and it will give you strength and impetus. Do not let life's irritants get the better of you. Do not explode. Know how to discharge that extra steam in a useful way.

Feed you fires. Take care of your physical health. Take care of your emotional well-being. Have something exciting to anticipate. Use the power of thought to excite and arouse your fire. Use it to empower your life.

(viii) Find the golden thread of greatness that runs through the world. Hunt for it. Search for it. Learn it. Prepare and adapt yourself always to live in a great way.

(ix) Search for role models, and pattern yourself on them. Be a role model to others.

Read this book again, and be great.

I wish you success and everything of the best!